←···· INTENSIVE DISCIPLES ····→

KNOWING GOD'S HEART

Missions and Evangelism

VINNIE CARAFANO
with KRISTIN CARAFANO

YWAM PUBLISHING
Seattle, Washington

YWAM Publishing is the publishing ministry of Youth With A Mission (YWAM), an international missionary organization of Christians from many denominations dedicated to presenting Jesus Christ to this generation. To this end, YWAM has focused its efforts in three main areas: (1) training and equipping believers for their part in fulfilling the Great Commission (Matthew 28:19), (2) personal evangelism, and (3) mercy ministry (medical and relief work).

For a free catalog of books and materials, call (425) 771–1153 or (800) 922–2143. Visit us online at www.ywampublishing.com.

Knowing God's Heart: Missions and Evangelism

Published by YWAM Publishing
a ministry of Youth With A Mission
P.O. Box 55787, Seattle, WA 98155-0787

Library of Congress Cataloging-in-Publication Data
Carafano, Vinnie.
    Knowing God's heart : missions and evangelism / Vinnie Carafano, with Kristin Carafano.
        pages cm — (Intensive discipleship course)
    ISBN 978-1-57658-520-7
    1. Missions—Study and teaching. 2. Evangelistic work—Study and teaching. 3. Church work with youth. I. Title.
    BV2090.C28 2013
    266—dc23   2013017056

Some names throughout this book have been changed to protect privacy.

First printing 2013

Printed in the United States of America

INTENSIVE DISCIPLESHIP COURSE

Developing Godly Character

Being Useful to God Now

Reaching a Lost World: Cults and World Religions

Knowing God's Heart: Missions and Evangelism

To the thousands of young people who have come with us over the past thirty-two years on mission outreaches all over the world. May the Lord of the harvest direct your lives to fulfill your destiny, touching the nations with His love.

CONTENTS

RESOURCES

FOREWORD

God has repeatedly called on teenagers throughout history to provide righteous, courageous leadership that has saved the people from destruction. The Intensive Discipleship Course materials provide a biblically based means to effectively equip the Davids and Esthers of our time, reinforcing their capacity to overcome today's giants and extend the kingdom of God throughout their communities and nations.

I deeply appreciate the diligence, wisdom, and sensitivity with which Vinnie and Jodie Carafano have faithfully invested in many young people for the past thirty-plus years in the context of local churches, mission outreaches, and communities at large. One of the main reasons for the Carafanos' effectiveness has been the strong biblical foundations they have been instrumental in nurturing within young lives. This, together with their understanding of how to help young people develop life disciplines that integrate these dynamic truths into all of life, provides an experience-rich backdrop, making the Intensive Discipleship Course series a particularly valuable training resource for any Christian youth worker, teacher, pastor, or parent.

May those who use these materials discover time-tested keys to unlocking the God-intended potential of their youth.

DALE KAUFFMAN
Founder and President, King's Kids International

PREFACE

Knowing God's Heart: Missions and Evangelism is a book for teenage and young adult Christians who have moved beyond the milk of God's Word (Isaiah 28:9–10) and are ready for a challenge. Just as the earlier books in the Intensive Discipleship Course dealt with character development, ministry training, and the study of world religions and cults in an intensive Bible-study format, this volume deals with the mission of the church in the same manner.

This book is about destiny, purpose, and calling. It directs readers to a life of fulfilling the plans of God and the purpose for which He created them. *Knowing God's Heart* calls for death to self and a higher reason for living than what most believers find. This is not a primer for baby Christians but an appeal for disciples to lay down their lives and take up the cross.

> Deliver those who are drawn toward death,
> And hold back those stumbling to the slaughter.
> If you say, "Surely we did not know this,"
> Does not He who weighs the hearts consider it?
> He who keeps your soul, does He not know it?
> And will He not render to each man according to his deeds?
> (Proverbs 24:11–12)

Studying missions is a dangerous thing. It means you have more responsibility to take action. Sometimes it's easier not to know . . . but would you prefer ignorance? If God's heart breaks, knowing that millions die each year without a relationship with His Son, would you rather know this and share in God's heart or miss out on what is so important to Him?

May the Lord use this book to send forth laborers into His harvest. May readers gain vision for the poor, widows, orphans, street children, the homeless, the unlovely, and the lonely. May we see past the outward facade of the seemingly successful and into their empty hearts. May we show His compassion to a broken world.

VINNIE CARAFANO

What Is the Intensive Discipleship Course?

How the Course Began

From 1980 to 1994 I was the youth pastor in a large nondenominational church. In 1986 I realized that it was impossible to give one message at our high-school and college-age group that would meet the needs of all the different kinds of people who came. We had totally devoted, radically sold out, on-fire, holy, dynamic, soul-winning kids, but we also had unsaved, doing-drugs, criminal-record, topless-dancer, drive-by-shooting-gang-member, Satan-worshiping, lost kids. Then there were those kids in the middle. How in the world could I present a message from the Word that could affect everyone there?

Most youth groups face the same dilemma. I developed this course to meet the needs of Christian students in high school and college who have a desire to grow in their relationship with the Lord and who need more in-depth discipling than we could do at youth group meetings. The foundational or evangelistic messages the rest of the group needed just weren't enough to challenge them. Since the first year we offered the Intensive Discipleship Course (referred to from here on as IDC), we saw a huge increase in the number of students who developed into leaders of their peers and became bold and dynamic examples of what a Christian student should be. Our goal is to produce disciples who are equipped with the power of God to fulfill His purposes throughout the world.

Who Should Do IDC?

Everybody who is hungry to know God more is invited to do IDC. Although the course is designed for young people age fifteen through college age, even adults (including pastors and youth leaders) who have taken the course say it has done a lot for their walk with the Lord. Setting aside time to focus on spiritual growth will benefit anyone who will stick to it.

Learning God's Truth

IDC will increase your understanding of the Lord and His plan for your life as you see what He says in the Bible about the priorities that are most important to Him.

Be diligent to present yourself approved to God, a worker who does not need to be ashamed, rightly dividing the word of truth. (2 Timothy 2:15)

All Scripture is given by inspiration of God, and is profitable for doctrine, for reproof, for correction, for instruction in righteousness, that the man of God may be complete, thoroughly equipped for every good work. (2 Timothy 3:16–17)

The Need for a Mentor

The dictionary defines a mentor as a wise and trusted person. One of the major components of IDC is spending time with an older and more spiritually mature person who can help you grow in the Lord. In choosing your mentor, look for someone who has a relationship with the Lord that you admire, a person you could confide in, someone easy to get along with and not too busy to spend an hour or so with you each week. This could be one of your parents or a grandparent, your pastor or youth leader, or someone else in your church whom you respect. If you are a teenager, ask your parents whom they would suggest and don't choose a mentor they do not approve of. (Some parents may not be believers and may not support your spiritual growth. In this case, it's fine to choose a mentor with the help of church leadership.) We urge you not to try to do IDC by yourself—the accountability to another person will help you stick to the course and process the work the Holy Spirit is doing in your life. Guys need to choose a man, and girls should choose a woman if at all possible, but your parents may approve of someone of the opposite sex. All of us—even adults—need mentors. If you are an adult or a college student, obviously you don't need parental permission in choosing a mentor, but it's wise to choose prayerfully. When you've found someone you would like to ask to be your mentor, make an appointment to see him or her and show the person your IDC book. Have the potential mentor read the section of this book called "Mentoring an Intensive Discipleship Course Student." You may want to leave the book with the potential mentor for a couple of days so that he or she really understands what IDC is. Make sure the mentor understands the commitment he or she is making to you and has the time to follow through with it. This is especially important with busy church staff members. If the person agrees, fill out the Course Commitment form on pages 23–24, sign it, and have your parents (if you are a teenager) and your mentor sign it.

Each week when you meet with your mentor, you'll show him or her the study you have done and talk about what you are learning. Make a commitment to be open and vulnerable about personal situations in your life. Since your mentor is a wise and trusted person, be honest about the victories and the needs in your life. If something comes up partway through IDC and your mentor can't follow through on his or her commitment, you can still complete the course and learn a lot from it. Don't give up!

Course Requirements

Weekly teachings. During the twelve-week course, you'll complete one study each week. Don't wait until the last minute, but do a little each day and let the teaching sink in. Each of the twelve teachings focuses on aspects of knowing the Lord and fulfilling His will. The margins next to the teachings will allow you to write down thoughts and questions and anything the Lord shows you during your times of study.

Whenever you see Scripture references throughout the text, look them up and write them *in your own words* on the lines provided. This will cause you to think through what each verse means and not simply copy a verse that you might not understand.

Daily Bible reading. In this fourth book of

the IDC, you will continue reading the Old Testament where the third book, *Reaching a Lost World,* left off. If you are doing this book without having completed the previous three books, we recommend that you do not use this schedule but begin reading three to four chapters of the New Testament daily. (An alternate Bible Reading Plan is provided for this on page 173.)

If you read the Bible for about fifteen minutes each day, you can finish it in one year. Just keep at it. If you miss a day or get behind, try to catch up. Check off each day after you have read the chapters, and start where you left off the next day. Be sure to read a translation of the Bible that you can understand. The New King James Version and the New International Version are highly recommended. Each week you can mark passages that you find confusing and ask questions at the next meeting with your mentor. If you have been reading somewhere else in the Old Testament or in the New Testament when the course begins, we suggest you put that study on hold for the duration of the course.

Scripture memory. Each week you'll memorize two verses or brief Bible passages. You don't have to get every word exactly. Have a clear grasp of the verse and memorize it as closely as you can. We suggest that you write out the verses on a piece of paper or 3 x 5 card and carry it with you. Read the verses throughout the week. It's not hard to memorize Scripture with enough repetition, but don't just memorize it as a parrot would, getting all the words right but having no idea what it means.

Prayer. Just as Jesus' disciples asked Him to teach them to pray, we need to learn to have an effective prayer life. The fifteen-minutes-per-morning requirement shown on the course commitment form is only about one percent of our daily lives, and yet many Christians don't spend that much time each day giving God their undivided attention. Once you begin at this level, it won't be long before you're thinking of more things to pray about and spending more time each day with the Lord.

Fasting. Fasting builds spiritual discipline. You may have never fasted before except between meals, and then only if it was absolutely necessary. Believe it or not, you can actually survive for a day without food. Just look at the people in the Bible who fasted for forty days. Each month you'll pick a day to fast when your schedule isn't packed. Be sure to drink lots of liquids. You'll find that if you start feeling weak and hungry, your strength will come back if you'll pray. I always fast before important spiritual events, such as a youth camp or missions trip, and whenever I'm really burdened with a personal need or a problem in the life of someone I care about. God comes through when we seek Him with our whole heart. Your mentor will be able to explain more about fasting.

Caution: Not everyone should participate in fasting. People who have health conditions or are taking medication should consult their physician about whether they should fast. All teenage students should discuss fasting with a parent and make sure that that parent is aware of the days of a fast.

Evaluations. On the first day of the course you will evaluate your spiritual condition as it relates to God's plan for your life by filling out the questionnaire on page 28. On the last day of the course you will fill out the questionnaire on page 148, evaluating each area you studied to discover what you learned. You will then be able to compare the two questionnaires so that you can chart your growth.

Mission report. Using *Operation World* by Jason Mandryk or another Christian missions resource, you will fill out the Mission Report page (during week 4) on a nation that interests you. Pray for the nation regularly, and don't be surprised if concern for its people grows in your heart to the extent that the Lord calls you to go there to serve Him. This is exactly what happened to me with the nation of India. Beginning

in Bible school in the early 1980s, I prayed for India as part of a class assignment, and I've ended up there three times so far, with plans to return.

Book reports. During IDC you'll be reading two nonfiction books from the following list. You can read other books if you like, but these are some of the best. It's easy for people to let their minds wander during a teaching, but a good story keeps everyone's attention. Lots of students who hate reading have told me that they can't put these books down, and many parents have read the books because their students in IDC had said that the books were so powerful.

- Corrie ten Boom, *The Hiding Place*
- Elisabeth Elliot, *Through Gates of Splendor*
- Loren Cunningham, *Is That Really You, God?*
- Brother Andrew, *God's Smuggler*
- Bruce Olson, *Bruchko*
- Don Richardson, *Lords of the Earth*
- Don Richardson, *Peace Child*
- Sister Gulshan Esther, *The Torn Veil*
- Jackie Pullinger, *Chasing the Dragon*

The book report forms are included in the appropriate places in the twelve-week course. (Book one should be read by week 5, and book two should be read by week 9.) The book report is a time to tell what you learned through reading the book and how it affected your relationship with the Lord. The ways God has used the people in the books will amaze you and will challenge you to step out in faith for God to use you as well.

You can order these books through any Christian bookstore. To save money, you may want to see if you can borrow them from your pastor or the church library. After reading them you'll agree they are so inspiring that you'll want to have your own copies. You will find a list of other useful books at the end of the course. I encourage you to continue reading great Christian books.

You'll notice that the books listed above are

missionary stories. Every Christian needs to know about missions. Even if you know that God has not called you to go to another country to preach the gospel, He has called you to participate in the Great Commission that Jesus gave to all Christians (Matthew 28:18–20). If you're interested in missions or have heard God's call to the mission field, be sure to read the fascinating book *Operation World* by Jason Mandryk. The book covers every country in the world and tells what God is doing there.

Spend a little time looking through it and read about countries that interest you—places you'd like to go, the country your ancestors came from, or places you've gone on vacation. Then think about the needs there: What if you lived in China, where Christians are still martyred, or Ethiopia, where the annual income is $333? Or Afghanistan, where there are 48,000 Muslim mosques but not one single Christian church? Take time to ask God to bring His kingdom to the ends of the earth.

TV and movie reports. Another goal in IDC is for you to examine your TV and movie viewing habits and find out what the Lord thinks about the things you watch. We don't believe that all TV and movies are evil or that it is a sin to watch movies and TV in general. The course commitment doesn't require students to avoid all TV or movies; it only asks students to write a brief report about what they do watch. Just the fact that you are accountable to your mentor and that you'll be writing reports might keep you from watching things you already know in your heart the Lord would not approve of. We want you to grow in discernment and not take for granted areas of your life that the Lord may want to change. Many Christians never stop to seek God's will in the areas of entertainment and recreation. You can watch anything you like, but if you do seek God's will about what you watch, you will be viewing it from the Lord's perspective. Then you will let *Him* decide whether it is something you

should be spending your time and devotion on. (Please read "Changing Your Viewing Habits" beginning on page 14 for further discussion of this course requirement.)

Additional course requirements. In addition to completing the previous course requirements, you are encouraged to (1) attend church weekly, including Sunday morning services and any youth/college group, (2) spend at least fifteen minutes in prayer every morning, (3) tithe (give 10 percent of all your income to God's work), and (4) surrender to the lordship of Christ, which means being obedient to Him and not holding back any part of your life from Him.

Course evaluation. Please write us using the course evaluation form at the back of the book and tell us what you thought about IDC. Your opinions will help us improve future editions of the course. We also really want to hear how the Lord used IDC in your life.

Course duration. IDC is designed to be used for twelve consecutive weeks. A September–December or January–April session is best, as straddling the Christmas holidays might cause you to lose momentum.

Don't skip the prerequisites! The book you are holding is the fourth in the series. The first IDC volume, *Developing Godly Character,* deals with basic issues of personal discipleship and lays the foundation for the second volume, *Being Useful to God Now,* which teaches how to be the kind of person God can work through. Then book three, *Reaching a Lost World,* helps you understand the beliefs and worldviews outside of our Christian faith. Unless you have allowed the dealings of God in your life that come as a result of IDC 1, you will not be spiritually prepared for IDC 2 or 3. For example, there is no use trying to teach people how to witness for the Lord unless they have made a decision to yield their lives fully to the lordship of Jesus. They might listen politely to the teaching, but they won't take action, because being known as a Christian could be detrimental to their social life and popularity with peers. The decision to die to self is part of the foundation that will make ministry training effective and cause you to care about this lost world rather than just study about it in a purely academic sense. If you really are prepared to seek God's plan for your life, then by all means, dive in!

The Content of This Volume

Knowing God's Heart: Missions and Evangelism is not designed to be read quickly. It's a twelve-week exercise in building and developing a foundational perspective so that we view our lives the way the Lord does. The process includes dying to our own wills, seeing people from God's point of view, understanding this life as it relates to eternity, and choosing to make necessary changes in our plans. Each day of completing a chapter and each week of processing it will mold the open-hearted reader more into the image of Jesus (Romans 12:2). By the end of twelve weeks, you'll look at the Lord, your own life, and other people differently.

Changing Your Viewing Habits

Do your viewing habits need to change? Maybe. If you recognize that sitting in front of a screen and passively absorbing endless hours of the world's values is having a negative effect on your relationship with the Lord, it's time for you to evaluate your habits. When we click through the TV channels or go to Netflix, we may not find anything that really appeals to us, but we've already planned to set aside time to watch something. We end up watching the least objectionable thing we can find, not necessarily something good. In this way, we squander a great deal of time. Have you ever finished watching a movie and then thought, *That was a total waste of two hours!* In the same way, the addictive nature of playing video games and surfing the Internet makes these activities an incredible time drain.

IDC might help you realize that you've been spending twenty to thirty hours (the US average) in front of a TV or computer or at the theater each week, but you have "never had enough time" to read the Bible. Think of all the other things in addition to reading the Bible that you could do with the extra time:

- Reach out to someone who needs a friend
- Improve your grades
- Work out
- Invest your life in discipling others
- Read a good book
- Learn the Bible
- Start a hobby
- Play sports
- Pray
- Help your mom or dad if you live at home
- Get more involved in church

Here are some helpful questions to evaluate TV shows, movies, video games, and Internet browsing:

1. Do you have aftereffects from things you have watched in the past that stir up temptations to sin? We've all had experiences of some recurring thought from the media: a gross or disgusting scene, a fear-producing image, a sensual or explicit picture. Different things will make different people stumble, depending on the weak areas in each person's life. The Lord already knows whether the movie that you'd like to see has elements that will tempt you to sin. Will you ask Him in advance if He wants you to see it? More important, will you obey what He tells you?

2. Have you ever regretted seeing a movie because of these effects? If so, will you ask God to help you stay away from anything that you'll regret later?

3. When we disobey the Lord, we disappoint Him. If God doesn't approve of your seeing a particular movie or TV show, how much of your fellowship and intimacy with God are you going

to lose if you do so anyway? If you're ministering to others, how much of the anointing of God will you give up in exchange for that movie? Of course, we know that God will forgive us if we repent later, but aren't we abusing the grace of God to sin with the plan of asking forgiveness afterward?

4. God intends for us to remain in constant fellowship with Him. Will that movie or TV program cause you to live in a world without God for an hour or two?

5. Does the program ridicule God, people who believe in Him, the authority of parents, and the holiness of sex in marriage? Does it slowly whittle away the foundations of what you believe? Situation comedies are especially guilty of this. They make us take lightly the things God takes seriously. We laugh at evil, and it doesn't seem so evil anymore. Does the movie lie to you about the way God made the universe? Does it deny the law of reaping what we sow or the fact that this life is temporary and eternity never ends?

Fools mock at sin. (Proverbs 14:9)

Neither filthiness, nor foolish talking, nor coarse jesting, which are not fitting, but rather giving of thanks. (Ephesians 5:4)

6. Do you hide behind the deception that since you are so strong in the Lord, the things that cause others to stumble won't affect you? There are some things that God simply doesn't want us to see or hear.

I will behave wisely in a perfect way. Oh, when will You come to me? I will walk within my house with a perfect heart. I will set nothing wicked before my eyes; I hate the work of those who fall away; it shall not cling to me. A perverse heart shall depart from me; I will not know wickedness. (Psalm 101:2–4)

Turn away my eyes from looking at worthless things, and revive me in Your way. (Psalm 119:37)

These things that God wants us to avoid include the following:

- Horror movies that glorify evil, exalt the kingdom of darkness, and make God seem either powerless or completely absent. Horror movies are a fantasy about the world the way Satan would like it to be if it weren't for the restraining hand of God.
- Sensual and suggestive comments that create mental images of sexual sin.
- Explicit or implied sexual scenes, which filmmakers design to cause you to identify with one of the people involved. God didn't make that beautiful girl or handsome guy for you to lust over. What you are seeing in a bedroom scene should be reserved for that person's spouse. For anyone else to view him or her in that way is sin.

7. How's the language? We know that God's name deserves respect. Is the language crude, offensive, disgusting? What does the Lord think about it? Hearing a lot of profanity makes it much easier for those words to come to mind when we stub our toe, drop something that breaks, or become frustrated. Are you conditioning your mind to react with impatience and anger rather than to look to the Lord when things don't go smoothly?

8. The Bible contains lots of violence, but the media have a way of lingering on the gruesome results of violence rather than simply telling the story. Are you watching sensationalized, gory violence? Does it cheapen the value of human life in your eyes? Does it train your mind to think that violence is an appropriate response to others?

9. Will you be courageous enough to be the one among your Christian friends who says no to certain movies, who gets up and walks out of the theater, who insists on changing the channel? This may be costly in terms of your immediate reputation, but it will gain you respect as one who takes following the Lord seriously and will bring conviction to those who aren't listening to their consciences. You see, the Holy Spirit is trying to bring to them the same sense of His disapproval over an ungodly movie or game.

You shall not follow a crowd to do evil. (Exodus 23:2)

The sinners in Zion are afraid; fearfulness has seized the hypocrites: "Who among us shall dwell with the devouring fire? Who among us shall dwell with everlasting burnings?" He who walks righteously and speaks uprightly . . . who stops his ears from hearing of bloodshed, and shuts his eyes from seeing evil: he will dwell on high; his place of defense will be the fortress of rocks; bread will be given him, his water will be sure. Your eyes will see the King in His beauty; they will see the land that is very far off. (Isaiah 33:14–17)

may or may not choose to ask their parents to be their mentor. Don't feel rejected if your children ask someone else. This is a natural part of the maturing process for a student. Parents can still be involved through prayer and encouragement and by asking questions and reading the book-report books.

Important Note: Please be aware that one of the course commitments is for students to fast one day per month. Some people, because of health conditions or medication, should not participate in fasting. Please discuss fasting with your son or daughter and know specifically when he or she goes on a fast. If you have any questions or concerns about the appropriateness of fasting for your son or daughter, please contact your physician.

IDC is a proven method of spiritual growth. Previous versions of this course have gone across America and to every continent. The course is demanding, but it follows the necessary steps for producing strong disciples. We feel that the church needs to challenge today's youth. The requirements of the course will stretch young people spiritually and teach them responsibility, faithfulness, and ways to set and achieve goals. We urge parents to be involved in IDC with their sons and daughters. One course requirement is for students to choose a mentor, and students

MENTORING AN INTENSIVE DISCIPLESHIP COURSE STUDENT

It is an honor when a young person interested in taking the Intensive Discipleship Course (IDC) chooses you to be his or her mentor. It shows that the person has a great deal of respect for you and sees in you a relationship with the Lord that is worthy of imitation. This intensive twelve-week course focuses on the personal discipleship that takes place between a student and a mentor. IDC contains a solidly evangelical perspective and focuses on the Lord Jesus Christ and young people's relationship with Him.

IDC is a demanding course, but Christian young people need a radical challenge. Powerful results in the lives of hundreds of students over the past two decades show the value of this approach. Any young person who wants to play on a school sports team, perform in a band, or excel in any field must diligently apply effort to the endeavor. Unfortunately, in Christian circles all we usually ask of young people is consistent attendance at our meetings. We, the creators of IDC, believe it is also necessary to call young people to diligence, faithfulness, self-discipline, and responsibility in their relationship with the Lord. We believe as well that young people will rise to the occasion if we encourage and support them.

We urge you to look through this material carefully and be sure that you have the time to fulfill the commitment you are making by agreeing to be a mentor. To disciple a young person in this way will undoubtedly take an effort on your part to free up time in your schedule, but the rewards will definitely be worth it.

YOUR ROLE AS A MENTOR

Your role as a mentor is different from that of a schoolteacher. You won't need to correct papers, read many reports, or give grades. Instead, your primary job will be to be available, to be open and honest with the student about your own walk with God, and to help him or her walk through a process of study and spiritual growth. You'll meet with your student each week for one to two hours.

Each week students work through a teaching designed to challenge their knowledge of Scripture and stimulate their walk with Jesus. They will be searching the Bible for truth to change their hearts. Each week your student will memorize two Scripture passages and will recite them to you. The student will also turn in two brief book reports during the course. Sometimes the student will have written TV or movie reports. You can briefly look at the student's Daily Bible Reading chart at the beginning of each teaching to make sure that the student is keeping up with the reading. Daily Bible reading should bring up questions that your student can write down on the chart and ask you to explain. Don't be afraid to say that you don't know the answer: Scripture contains plenty of passages that mystify all of us. You might suggest other Scriptures or recommend Christian books on a particular subject. You may want to present both sides of a controversial topic. Perhaps the best answer to a question you can't answer is, "Let's try to find out together."

Asking your student questions to stimulate his or her seeking the Lord to find the answer is preferable to handing out the answer. In discipling young people, we must be careful to avoid encouraging them to depend on us for answers. Our job as leaders is to be facilitators of learning rather than spiritual gurus. We don't have all the answers, and we must make this clear to the young people while pointing them to the One who does have all the answers. We are to let them find their own revelation from God's Word as we help them know the Holy Spirit as their teacher.

But the anointing which you have received from Him abides in you, and you do not need that anyone teach you; but as the same anointing teaches you concerning all things, and is true, and is not a lie, and just as it has taught you, you will abide in Him. (1 John 2:27)

"But the Helper, the Holy Spirit, whom the Father will send in My name, He will teach you all things, and bring to your remembrance all things that I said to you." (John 14:26)

You must be willing to help your student wrestle through difficulties and painful but necessary changes without allowing an unhealthy dependency on you. It is frequently the tendency of those with a shepherd's heart to try to make life easy for their flock, sometimes blunting the sharp edges of God's Word in the process. Yet you must allow the Lord to deal with your student and not abort the process of conviction in his or her life.

A mentor's message, though always spoken with compassion and love, must be "Here is truth—what are you and the Lord going to do about it?" Students will respond in one of three ways. One response is to feel miserable and condemned, which can lead some to hardening their hearts. We must steer them past this obstacle, giving hope that the grace of God will transform them. A second response is to try to improve, which results in legalism, performance orientation, and either spiritual pride or more condemnation. Again, we must steer students toward genuine heart change. A third response is the one we desire—lasting transformation by the work of the Holy Spirit.

You will not need to personally oversee some of the other parts of the student's commitment, such as tithing, church attendance, fasting, or daily prayer. The student is on the honor system for those aspects of the course.

The Personal Touch in Discipleship

Building a relationship in which your student feels comfortable in revealing personal thoughts, feelings, and needs is essential. Your interest and questions can draw the student into being open with you. Trust and confidentiality are part of the foundation for discipling a young person, who may entrust you with deep hurts, secrets, or confessions of sin. You'll need to use great care and wisdom to decide whether or not to disclose such matters and, if so, how to discuss them with the student's parents.

Don't be afraid to be honest with the young

person you are discipling. If God could use only people who had everything worked out in their lives, I would certainly be disqualified, and probably you would be too. I've found that being vulnerable and open about my weaknesses allows students to feel confident in discussing their struggles. On the other hand, a leader who gives the appearance of having it all together can intimidate young people, causing them to fear being rejected, judged, or condemned if they confess sins or areas of weakness. Let's be careful to create an environment where openness and honesty prevail (Proverbs 28:13).

During the week, we urge you to pray for your student and listen for insights from the Lord to bring up the next time you meet with the student. Each week when you meet together, be sure to close in prayer to take before the Lord the specific needs of the student and the area of teaching the student is studying.

Either you or the student you are discipling may have an extra busy week or have to miss your meeting for another reason, such as vacation, illness, or final exams. As soon as possible, reschedule the meeting so that he or she doesn't lose momentum. If the student falls behind and hasn't completed the week's assignments by the day of your meeting, don't cancel the meeting. You can still talk and pray together. Encourage the student to catch up as soon as possible and follow up to see that the student does so. Many students need adult help in carrying through with their commitments.

We suggest a graduation ceremony or celebration of some kind for the student upon completion of the course. Include parents, family, and friends. Award a diploma to commend the student for the work done. This is a great way to recognize the student publicly when he or she has completed the course. Speak of the student's accomplishments in a way that will encourage others to take bold steps of spiritual growth. This can be a good witness to the church that some

students are godly and dedicated to walking with the Lord. It may also be convicting for some of the church members, including other young people.

The Goal of Discipleship: Looking Beyond IDC

The result of the process of discipleship should be that disciples become disciplers. The following scripture outlines three phases in this process:

For Ezra had prepared his heart TO SEEK *the Law of the Lord, and* TO DO *it, and* TO TEACH *statutes and ordinances in Israel. (Ezra 7:10; emphasis added)*

The first step is seeking and learning God's ways. Next comes living out what we have learned. Finally, we teach others His ways. The order here is crucial, and all three steps are necessary for discipleship to be complete. Some people try to live the Christian life without a genuine understanding of it and end up inventing their own versions of Christianity. Others try to teach what they haven't worked out in their own lives and sometimes bring reproach on the Lord and the church. Still others seek and do but never teach, and the chain of events from the patriarchs through the cross and the church finds a dead end in their lives: they never pass the gospel on to others. As leaders of young people, we need to aim their spiritual lives in such a way that the truth we pass on to them continues to affect the world for generations to come.

And the things that you have heard from me among many witnesses, commit these to faithful men who will be able to teach others also. (2 Timothy 2:2)

Pastors and Youth Leaders with Multiple Students

One option for a pastor or youth leader is to have several students take the course at the same time and meet for discipleship and mentoring in a small group. Be sure not to let this group become too large, or the personal nature of it will be lost. We recommend no more than five young people at a time in a small group. If you have many young people you would like to have take the course, either raise up other qualified small-group leaders or teach the course in a large group with smaller discussion groups. Follow the same course guidelines as for mentors with one student.

STUDENT PROGRESS CHART

Here is a chart to help you keep track of your student's progress through the course. Check the appropriate box when the student has completed each assignment.

Week	Scriptures Memorized	Daily Bible Reading	Teaching and Study Questions Completed	Assignments Due
1				Self-Evaluation 1
2				
3				
4				Mission Report
5				Book Report 1
6				
7				
8				
9				Book Report 2
10				
11				
12				Self-Evaluation 2 & Course Evaluation

Mentor's Course Evaluation

We value your input! When the student has completed *Knowing God's Heart*, please take a few minutes to give us your suggestions and comments about the course.

Name:

Address:

Phone: E-mail:

Name of student(s):   Age of student(s):

Dates of course:

1. Please rate the following on a scale of 1 to 10, with 10 as the best rating:

	1	2	3	4	5	6	7	8	9	10
• Quality of content and presentation	1	2	3	4	5	6	7	8	9	10
• Ease of use	1	2	3	4	5	6	7	8	9	10
• Practical value of teachings	1	2	3	4	5	6	7	8	9	10
• Effect of the course on the student	1	2	3	4	5	6	7	8	9	10
• Format of the book	1	2	3	4	5	6	7	8	9	10

2. What were the strongest points of the course?

3. What were the weakest points?

4. What part of the course or experience was most encouraging?

5. What, if any, other topics would you like to have seen covered?

6. Other suggestions for improvement?

Thanks for your help!
Please photocopy and mail to
Vinnie Carafano, 936 W Sunset Rd., El Paso, TX 79922

COURSE COMMITMENT FORM

Carefully read and fill out this course commitment after discussing the course with your parents (if you are a teenager) and your mentor and after receiving their approval to go ahead.

Name: Age:

Mentor's Name:

Please answer the following three questions on another sheet of paper:
1. How did you become a Christian, and how is your relationship with the Lord now?
2. Why do you want to participate in the Intensive Discipleship Course?
3. What are your goals in your relationship with Jesus?

You are about to enter a time of great spiritual growth. This statement of commitment will show your decision to the Lord, your parents, your mentor, and yourself that you have set aside the next three months to focus on seeking God, doing those things that will help you grow in Him, and being accountable to spiritual leadership.

I commit to do the following:
1. Complete all twelve sessions of the course.
2. Read a portion of the Old Testament.
3. Read two of the recommended books and write a one-page report on each book.
4. Attend church weekly—Sunday morning and youth/college group.
5. Memorize twenty-four assigned Scripture verses.
6. Fast one designated day each month.
7. Spend at least fifteen minutes in prayer every morning.
8. Tithe (give 10 percent of all my income to God's work).
9. Surrender to the lordship of Christ, which means being obedient to Him and not holding back any part of my life from Him.
10. Research and write a one-page mission report on the nation of my choice.

I will be accountable to do the following:
1. Keep up, or improve, the school grades I am earning now.
2. Put ungodly influences out of my life:
   - For the next twelve weeks I will listen only to Christian music.
   - For any movie or TV show I watch (other than the news, sports, or documentaries) I will write a brief summary of the plot and comment on the movie or show from God's perspective.
3. Keep Jesus as my first love (Revelation 2:4). This includes putting aside dating relationships and romances for the next twelve weeks and setting the time apart to seek the Lord without being

Continued on next page…

distracted. Parents of a teenager and the mentor can make an exception to this commitment for a student dating another committed Christian before the course begins.

No one will be looking over your shoulder to see whether you are fulfilling these three commitments. The purpose of the commitments is to help you grow, and you will benefit from IDC according to the degree you are willing to enter into the spirit of it.

Don't overload your schedule. If you have a difficult semester load of classes or a job and take IDC, you won't be able to do your best in any of these areas. Prayerfully decide whether this is the right time for you to make this commitment and, if so, how you will rearrange your schedule.

Parent's Commitment (for teenagers)

I have read the course requirements and believe this is a valuable experience for my son or daughter. I will encourage my student in spiritual growth and pray for him or her daily.

_____

Mentor's Commitment

I have read the course requirements and believe this is a valuable experience for a Christian young person. I will encourage him or her in spiritual growth, meet each week for twelve weeks, and pray for him or her daily.

_____

Student's Commitment

I have read the requirements and know it will be tough, but I'm going to give the course my very best and become a man or woman of God. I'm ready for the challenge!

_____

INTRODUCTION

At this moment I'm thirty-six thousand feet over the Pacific, returning from a mission outreach in Asia. With reports scheduled at two churches the next two Sundays and others coming up soon afterward, the challenge for me is to communicate adequately to several thousand people the intensity of the past month: living in the jungle, preaching the gospel to two unreached tribal groups, eating strange food (including such delights as pig ear and bitter gourd), and taking bucket showers (in which one pours water of questionable purity over one's head with a ladle from a bucket that was filled when the water was last running).

The slideshow photos will help my audiences understand a little. People will gasp at the poverty, make appropriate sounds at the photos of adorable street children, and marvel at the stories of God's kingdom expanding. But despite the passion in my voice and the eloquence I'll try to bring, their grasp of the reality of the outreach will fall far short. They didn't smell the aromas of life in the Third World; see the tears of those asking for prayer or receiving the Lord; play with those sweet, runny-nosed, barefoot children; or pray constantly for safety and health for a team of twenty-nine young missionaries under my care.

They won't be able to fathom the experience of sleeping in a bamboo church and showing love to a poor pastor and his family who have none of the perks we have in Western ministry. They won't be

Obedient responder to God's direction for broken, lost, and desperate people. Must be willing to dream big and act faithfully. No prior experience necessary. Can begin immediately.

Today, there are seven billion people in the world. Out of this vast number,

- one in seven children is uneducated;

- 925 million people are hungry and malnourished (three times the population of the United States alone);
- 6.4 billion don't have a living relationship with Jesus.

Today, there are millions of children who have never slept in a bed, who fight to stay alive, and who live in fear of sex trafficking, kidnapping, and gangs. Today, there is an elderly neighbor who sits by himself, lonely and desperate for someone to talk to him. Today, there is a classmate struggling through a breakup, hungry for a reason to keep living. Today, most Christians will close their eyes.

Will anyone choose to see?

In response to the world's desperation, most people either turn away or become overwhelmed and think they could never make a difference. Sadly, many Christians live completely self-absorbed! They focus on personal needs and neglect both the huge, life-changing opportunities and the small, daily opportunities God gives them. Yet God isn't looking for spiritual giants; rather, He's looking for a believing, obedient heart who is willing to act faithfully every day.

In each of the following chapters, you'll see a "help wanted" section. These sections will highlight major world issues and then give you practical ways to get involved today. If something grabs at your heart, don't wait until tomorrow to do something about it! Choose to be the one who answers the call, lives faithfully, and actively carries out the tangible mercy that Jesus provides. Today, there's a world out there that needs someone to take that small step. Will it be you?

able to see the pastor's sacrificial zeal for the lost in his corner of the world. They won't have felt the joy of seeing the light go on in the face of a person who understands for the first time what Jesus did on the cross, and why. They won't have laid hands on the broken or heard the stories of the desperate.

They'll shake my hand at the end of the service, maybe put a check in the special offering, or pick up a newsletter. This is all good. But what I really want is for them to understand enough to bother them—to upset their priorities as they spend a monthly paycheck that surpasses that pastor's annual income, and maybe take another look at the many self-indulgences we all excuse in our daily lives in North America.

I hope that after hearing about others' lives around the world, they'll be more grateful for the lives of convenience they have always known. I hope they will urge their churches to increase missions giving, adopt a church in a nation filled with spiritual darkness, or fund the translation of the New Testament into a language in which it has never been read. I hope they'll stand behind a young missionary just getting started, remember to pray each day for a world outside their personal experience, and raise their kids to value the eternal more than the temporary.

I especially hope the youth listening to me will hear a call to lay down their lives for something much bigger than themselves. I hope they will become less interested in extreme sports and more interested in extreme needs. I hope they will commit their lives to serving the King who is worthy. I hope they will become everything that the Lord created them to be.

And I hope this book will lead *you* to know the heart of God and accomplish all of His purposes in your life.

SCRIPTURE MEMORY

Philippians 3:8–10
I have suffered the loss of all things, and count them as rubbish, that I may gain Christ and be found in Him, . . . that I may know Him and the power of His resurrection, and the fellowship of His sufferings, being conformed to His death.

Psalm 90:12
So teach us to number our days, that we may gain a heart of wisdom.

FILL OUT THE SELF-EVALUATION ON THE NEXT PAGE.

DAILY BIBLE READING

✓ Check when completed	
Sunday	Psalms 120–127
Monday	Psalms 128–134
Tuesday	Psalms 135–139
Wednesday	Psalms 140–145
Thursday	Psalms 146–150
Friday	Proverbs 1–4
Saturday	Proverbs 5–9

See the Daily Bible Reading section on page 11 about this and alternative Bible reading schedules.

BIBLE READING QUESTIONS/THOUGHTS

_____
_____
_____
_____
_____
_____
_____
_____
_____
_____
_____

PRAYER NEEDS THIS WEEK

_____
_____
_____
_____
_____
_____
_____
_____
_____
_____
_____

1

SELF-EVALUATION 1

Fill out this self-evaluation. At the end of the course you'll fill out the same evaluation and chart your spiritual growth.

1. My relationship with the Lord is

| *distant* | 1 | 2 | 3 | 4 | 5 | 6 | 7 | 8 | 9 | 10 | *intimate* |

2. My experience in sharing the gospel is

| *nonexistent* | 1 | 2 | 3 | 4 | 5 | 6 | 7 | 8 | 9 | 10 | *frequent* |

3. My love and concern for others is

| *weak* | 1 | 2 | 3 | 4 | 5 | 6 | 7 | 8 | 9 | 10 | *strong* |

4. My awareness of missions is

| *very little* | 1 | 2 | 3 | 4 | 5 | 6 | 7 | 8 | 9 | 10 | *very great* |

5. My understanding of God's plan for my life is

| *very little* | 1 | 2 | 3 | 4 | 5 | 6 | 7 | 8 | 9 | 10 | *very great* |

6. My willingness to make sacrifices for the kingdom of God is

| *nonexistent* | 1 | 2 | 3 | 4 | 5 | 6 | 7 | 8 | 9 | 10 | *sincere* |

Lesson one
TWO QUESTIONS TO ASK THE LORD

The book of Acts (or the Acts of the Apostles) describes the apostle Paul's incredible conversion experience on the road to Damascus, when he was still named Saul.

> Then Saul, still breathing threats and murder against the disciples of the Lord, went to the high priest and asked letters from him to the synagogues of Damascus, so that if he found any who were of the Way, whether men or women, he might bring them bound to Jerusalem.
>
> As he journeyed he came near Damascus, and suddenly a light shone around him from heaven. Then he fell to the ground, and heard a voice saying to him, "Saul, Saul, why are you persecuting Me?"
>
> And he said, "Who are You, Lord?"
>
> Then the Lord said, "I am Jesus, whom you are persecuting. It is hard for you to kick against the goads."
>
> So he, trembling and astonished, said, "Lord, what do You want me to do?"
>
> Then the Lord said to him, "Arise and go into the city, and you will be told what you must do."
>
> And the men who journeyed with him stood speechless, hearing a voice but seeing no one. Then Saul arose from the ground, and when his eyes were opened he saw no one. But they led him by the hand and brought him into Damascus. And he was three days without sight, and neither ate nor drank. (Acts 9:1–9)

This must be an important story, because it's found three times in the book of Acts (9:1–9; 22:6–11; 26:13–18). Each account gives a few different details. So let's look at this story, and specifically at Saul's two questions when he encounters the Lord for the first time.

WHO ARE YOU, LORD?

Saul was the greatest persecutor of the early church. His zeal to stamp out this new religion came from his belief that it drew the Jews away from the truth passed down from their ancestors and into a blasphemous new teaching that declared Jesus of Nazareth was the Son of God. Saul's spiritual pedigree showed the highest level of training and commitment to Judaism. As a strict Pharisee, he was the ideal tool of the chief priests and Pharisees to put an end to the rapidly growing band of followers of this crucified Messiah.

Philippians 3:4b–6

_____

_____

Acts 22:3–5

True Story

So that you can understand the background of this book and my motivation for writing it, come take a quick tour of our world on the mission field, to a few of the places where I've seen how lost and broken our world really is.

Let's go to India, where masses of fearful and superstitious Hindus who have never heard Jesus' name worship stone gods who don't answer their prayers . . . to Russia, with six hundred thousand orphans growing up in institutions without the love of a family, aimed toward drug addiction, crime, and prostitution when they are turned onto the streets at age eighteen . . . to South America, where ragged children sniff glue to quench their hunger pangs and dig through the trash for their next meal . . . to Ethiopia, where street kids are starving and selling their bodies for the going rate of thirty-six cents, often becoming infected with HIV in the process . . . or to the bustling cities of China, where the worship of ancestors or traditional gods is only a means to the end result of an insatiable pursuit of money. Maybe next we'll go to the grim scenes of misery in Haiti, where people live under the influence of witch doctors and gods of voodoo . . . to Mexican towns dominated by the violence of warring drug cartels . . . or to Thailand, where girls and boys sold into sex slavery satisfy the depravity of foreign tourists.

This world is so very lost without Jesus. Sufferings compounded by injustice, poverty, and the love of money cause untold sorrow. There's no lack of possible answers the Lord may give to one who dares to ask, "What do You want me to do, Lord?"

The arrogant Saul had authority to be the judge, jury, and executioner for the leaders of the Jews. He acted with confidence that he was doing the will of God. But in an instant both his plans and perspective on life changed as God stepped into his life unexpectedly. Saul was stunned. He knew it must be divine power that had knocked him off his horse and blinded him, but the identity of that divine power was in question. Saul was shocked and blinded— and maybe a little singed—as pride turned into terror in one second.

Whoever this was, Saul knew that this person couldn't be ignored. Before he even knew who he was talking to, he called out, "Lord"— not *higher power*, not *supreme being*, not *man upstairs*, but *Lord*. "Who are You, Lord?" The answer to Saul's first question must have been the most terrifying words he had ever heard. He had been after Jesus' followers, but now Jesus was after him! The Lord had Saul's full attention. Saul knew that Jesus could send a second lightning bolt to finish him off at any moment.

Let's note an important side issue before proceeding with Saul's life-altering experience. Jesus asked, "Why are you persecuting Me?" Saul had never even seen Jesus in person, much less taken part in Jesus' crucifixion. Saul's current actions of violence and anger were directed against Jesus' *followers*. But here he learned that Jesus takes it personally whenever His servants suffer for their faith. In fact, God has always felt the sufferings of His people.

Isaiah 63:9

Back to Saul's question. "Who are You, Lord?" isn't just Saul's question. It's also our question, and it sets a pattern for us to follow. It's not a question that we can ask once, get a quick answer, and then be done. We never can get a complete answer to this question—God is bigger than we are. Can we fit the God whose hand created the universe (Isaiah 48:13) into our puny human minds? The answer to the question is as big as God Himself.

Romans 11:33

_____

_____

Job 26:14

_____

_____

Have you known the Lord for five, ten, or twenty years? That's just the edge. Have you walked with God and think you understand Him? It's still just a whisper. There's always more. You can't exhaust spiritual growth. None of us has arrived yet. And when we've been in God's presence ten thousand years, we'll still be in awe as we find out more of who God is.

This question stayed on Saul's mind even after he became known as the apostle Paul. You can hear the wistfulness, the hunger for God, in his voice as he wrote the following verse.

Philippians 3:10

_____

_____

Notice that the verse doesn't say "the power of His resurrection _or_ the fellowship of His sufferings." It says _and_. We don't get to choose. These are two of the primary ways we get to know the Lord. Of course, we grow on a regular basis from our devotional times of prayer and Bible study as well as hearing good sermons from the pastor on Sundays, but there are times that our faith moves forward at an accelerated pace. Paul's mention of the power of Christ's resurrection speaks of the ways God shows His divine nature and glory, such as through answered prayer, unexpected breakthroughs, sovereign interventions, and miraculous acts. But then there's the second statement—the fellowship of His sufferings.

Have you ever thought you knew something about the Lord, but after you've been through a painful growth experience, you _really_ know it? Before our faith is stretched and tested, we say that God is faithful and God is good. At early stages of spiritual growth, however, this is more of a quotation of Scripture and the testimony of other believers than it is a heartfelt personal declaration. Then we go through times when we have nothing to cling to but God Himself, and we really grow. Simple aspects of God's character unfold to depths of truth, and we can say with certainty that God _is_ faithful and good. It becomes something we know in our hearts to be true, rather than a mental concept. It's experiential verification of the promises of Scripture.

"Who are You, Lord?" is a daily question. It is a daily quest to know Him, to understand His ways, to really get it. When we stop asking this question, we stop growing. We can easily slip into a season of apathy and dullness if we stop pursuing the knowledge of God. May we each cultivate a divine dissatisfaction with our current knowledge of the Lord and pursue increasing understanding of who He is.

Lord, What Do You Want Me to Do?

Now let's look at the second question. Saul, lying in the dust, voice quavering—and probably the rest of him quivering—asks, "Lord, what do You want me to do?" He was humbled and shaken. Still in shock that the Jesus whom he despised was the Lord who held his life in His hands, Saul changed his focus. Without a doubt, one of the motives for Saul's question was to see if he could do anything to obtain mercy rather than the clearly deserved judgment he expected. But I think there was more than self-preservation at play. Saul had believed he was doing the will of God as he tried to stamp out the early church. Although he was misguided, he wanted to know the will of God and fulfill it. Now was his chance to do it the right way.

Life was no longer about doing what he thought was best or what he wanted to do. Before this moment, Saul knew where he was going and what he was doing. Now everything was up in the air. You can hear in Saul's words his submission to One he recognizes as far greater. He makes no attempt to

Bible translator and/or funder for unreached people groups. Must have patience, commitment, and zeal in providing Scripture to people who have never heard the gospel.

If you are reading this Intensive Discipleship Course, it means that you have access to a Bible. In fact, you probably have unlimited ability to read the Bible—it's free on the Internet, always available on smartphones and tablets, sitting in bookstores, and playing on the radio. Before going any further, pause and thank God for the treasure of the Bible in your native language.

But think for a moment: what if those resources didn't exist? What if there weren't Scripture verses translated into your language and you couldn't sit down to open God's Word for yourself? What if there weren't churches because there wasn't Scripture to preach about? At this moment, there are

- 2,100 languages into which not a single Scripture verse has been translated;
- over 350 million people who speak those languages;
- numerous translation projects taking ten to twenty years to translate the New Testament alone.

Translating the Bible is a long and extremely tedious process, as a missionary must first travel to a remote part of the world, learn the language of the people while gaining an understanding of the culture, and then, in many cases, develop an alphabet for the language and teach the people how to read. Furthermore, there must be extensive revising and editing to ensure that

the gospel is translated to the new language with accuracy and clarity. However, we are living in a time where technology and opportunity for translation abounds—for example, since 1942, Wycliffe Bible Translators has successfully translated the Bible into 749 languages, affecting nearly 145 million people. The stories of indigenous people who have heard the gospel for the first time will explode your faith. To read one example, get ahold of the book *And the Word Came with Power* by Joanne Shetler.

It's Your World—Do Something Today!

Pray for a current Wycliffe translation team and encourage them by sending letters and financial support. Go to *www.wycliffe.org /pray/prayforawycliffemissionary .aspx* to get started today.

If Bible translation is something you feel passionate about, consider doing a summer internship with Wycliffe translators. Visit *www.wycliffenextgen.com* for more information.

negotiate. The proud and self-righteous Pharisee had met his Maker. Though he didn't know what the answer to his question would be, he knew he would have to obey. Saul had been the respected one, haughty and fearless as he persecuted the church. Now he submits to the One who is greater. The master of his fate becomes the servant.

Christ's answer to Saul included both the immediate and the long term. Saul heard instruction about where to go that day as well as what the Lord wanted him to do for the rest of his life (Acts 22:10; 26:16–18). If we ask the same question, we'll get the same type of answer. If we obey the small, immediate, or daily commands, they will continually point us to the long-term goal of God's destiny for our lives.

"Lord, what do you want me to do?" is another daily question. When we stop asking this question, we stop serving and stop bearing fruit. We can go through the motions of the Christian life and get in a real rut of meaningless and empty repetition. This leads to a boring Christian life—which should be an oxymoron! Serving the living God can't be boring!

Here's the way out. There's an old saying: "The more independent you are, the less you pray. The less independent you are, the more you pray." We need God to direct our lives, even in the smallest details. Seeking God, both for greater knowledge of who He is and for the unfolding of His plan, is worth every hour invested and all the effort we make. We can walk in divine wisdom to the extent that we ask for it and listen, and then do what God says. And the excitement of seeing God at work through us is unlike any other thing!

Psalm 90:12

_____

_____

_____

_____

True Story

At this moment I'm sitting in a large city in Kurdistan, Northern Iraq. The many mosques surrounding us have just called the faithful Muslims to prayer, as they do five times each day. The wailing calls of the muezzin aren't synchronized, so beginning at about 4:00 a.m. and repeating at each of the five daily prayer times, we hear the declaration that God is great. I wish the phrase were directed to the true and living God, the One who sent His Son to the earth to die for our sins, but that's not the case.

The culture of this city and nation is very religious. Most of the men hold small circles of prayer beads, much like a rosary, to remind them of the ninety-nine names of Allah. The mosques are architecturally magnificent and draw large crowds. People bring up Allah in everyday conversation with the phrase *inshallah*, "if God wills." Women are dressed according to their husband's or father's interpretation of the Koran (the Islamic holy book) and sharia (Islamic law). Some women wear head-to-toe black gowns, others wear long jackets with scarves to cover their hair, and some wear Western-style clothing.

There are some churches in defined Christian districts. Some are vibrant congregations with passionate worship, while others are relics of more spiritually alive ancestors. Persecution comes and goes, and most Christians, whether genuine believers or cultural followers, have already fled the country. From an earthly perspective, there are too few to sustain the faith in the face of such opposition, but God is not limited by numbers (1 Samuel 14:6).

Take a moment to pray for the Christians who live under the spiritual oppression of Islamic nations. Pray that they would be strong in the Lord, confident and unashamed. Pray for the many dissatisfied Muslims who are seeking spiritual truth as a result of the Holy Spirit's work in their hearts. Pray for the light of the gospel to shine in these very dark places.

Keeping Relationship First

Note the order of Saul's questions: "Who are You?" comes before "What do You want me to do?" Relationship comes before responsibilities. Until we know who God is, it makes no sense to ask what to do, because the unchanged heart is not inclined toward obedience. We must pursue the knowledge of God more than the work of God. The foundation of relationship can't be replaced with our own plans, effort, or reasoning. But once that foundation of a living relationship with the Savior is established and nourished in an ongoing lifestyle of love and worship, the next step becomes clear: making the knowledge of God that we experience available to a lost world. If we ask, "Lord, what do You want me to do?" the answer must include the lost world around—the people Jesus died to save.

God asks all of us the same question he asked the prophet Isaiah long ago.

Isaiah 6:8

_____

_____

"Who will go for Us?" Start as Saul did, by humbling yourself before the Lord, and God will direct your steps.

Wrap-up

Let's wrap this up and apply it to our lives. Let's put Saul's two questions into a fresh prayer that sums up all we have seen so far.

Father, I'm like Saul. I have my own plans, but they may be the complete opposite of Your plans for my life. I want to know You and understand why You created me. Help me not to be so stuck in the path I've set for my life that I miss Your path. Help me not to be so busy being busy that I don't take time to seek Your face and Your will. I ask, "What do You want me to do?" And I thank You for Your great love for me and for the whole world. In Jesus' name. Amen.

What stands out to you in this prayer?

_____

_____

What has God been saying to you this week?

_____

_____

How does this affect your daily life?

_____

_____

How does this affect your life plans?

_____

_____

DAILY BIBLE READING

SCRIPTURE MEMORY

Psalm 107:9
For He satisfies the longing
　　soul,
And fills the hungry soul with
　　goodness.

Psalm 138:3
In the day when I cried out,
　　You answered me,
And made me bold with
　　strength in my soul.

✔ Check when completed

Sunday	Proverbs 10–13
Monday	Proverbs 14–17
Tuesday	Proverbs 18–19
Wednesday	Proverbs 20–21
Thursday	Proverbs 22–24
Friday	Proverbs 25–29
Saturday	Proverbs 30–31

BIBLE READING QUESTIONS/THOUGHTS

_____
_____
_____
_____
_____
_____
_____
_____
_____
_____
_____

PRAYER NEEDS THIS WEEK

_____
_____
_____
_____
_____
_____
_____
_____
_____

2

WE REMAIN SILENT

The book of 2 Kings in the Old Testament tells the story of the king of Syria who besieged Samaria during a famine and of four unlikely messengers of God. This is real history, but we'll see how it is also a parable of our lives. You and I are in this story.

FOUR UNLIKELY MESSENGERS

The story starts with the Syrian army surrounding the walled city of Samaria.

> And it happened after this that Ben-Hadad king of Syria gathered all his army, and went up and besieged Samaria. And there was a great famine in Samaria; and indeed they besieged it until a donkey's head was sold for eighty shekels of silver, and one-fourth of a kab of dove droppings for five shekels of silver. (2 Kings 6:24–25)

The people of Samaria didn't have a chance against the enemy soldiers, so they locked the gates and holed up inside. No one could go in or out because of the siege, and they were running out of food. They had eaten all the crops that were stored up. The pantries were empty. The wagons and baskets at the market were bare. All the restaurants shut down.

Things got so desperate they were eating donkey heads and dove droppings. I don't know about you, but my stomach is really close to my heart, and that sounds awful. Does your mother have a good recipe for donkey heads? When you come home after a long day at school and head for the kitchen, how would you feel if *that* were on the stove? And dove droppings?

Then things got even worse. People turned to cannibalism and began eating their own children.

> Then, as the king of Israel was passing by on the wall, a woman cried out to him, saying, "Help, my lord, O king!"
>
> And he said, "If the LORD does not help you, where can I find help for you? From the threshing floor or from the winepress?" Then the king said to her, "What is troubling you?"
>
> And she answered, "This woman said to me, 'Give your son, that we may eat him today, and we will eat my son tomorrow.' So we boiled my son, and ate him. And I said to her on the next day, 'Give your son, that we may eat him'; but she has hidden her son." (2 Kings 6:26–29)

The final gasp of a dying culture is when it turns on its own children and destroys its future. But the story doesn't end there.

> Now there were four leprous men at the entrance of the gate; and they said to one another, "Why are we sitting here until we die? If we say, 'We will enter the city,' the famine is in the city, and we shall die there. And if we sit here, we die also. Now therefore, come, let us surrender to the army of the Syrians. If they keep us alive, we shall live; and if they kill us, we shall only die." (2 Kings 7:3–4)

In this desperate and dying city lived four men with leprosy who were also starving to death. Leprosy is a horrible and terrifying disease that results in parts of the body rotting away. On our mission trips to Panama we ministered at a leprosy community and saw deformed people with missing fingers. When we were in India in a primitive village, a sixteen-year-old girl came up to my wife, Jodie. She pointed to what looked like a rash on her ankle, so Jodie laid hands on her and started to pray. When

True Story

My retired missionary friend stood in our kitchen, sharing his burden for one of the unreached tribal groups in the Philippines. I was preoccupied and didn't really pay attention. A few months later he came back to visit and repeated the story of the Badjao Muslim people. This time it hit me hard, and I wondered how I could have missed the significance the first time he told me the story. Here's the point that struck me: the local people's nickname for the Badjao is "the godforsaken."

My soul rose up in protest against this unfair and untrue label. God cares about this tribe as much as any other group of people. We had already been in the Philippines on two outreaches, and I remembered the scrawny children begging in the streets, their normally dark hair streaked with lighter shades because of malnutrition. They weren't godforsaken, and I knew we had to do our part to tell them so. This burden resulted in two summers of productive missionary work with the Badjao, taking a combined total of forty-eight people there for five weeks each time. Here are a few stories from our newsletter reports:

"It's sad to see the Badjao people labeled a 'menace to sanitation' and an 'eyesore' in the newspapers there. I'm sure the Lord doesn't see them that way. We are finding open doors to minister in Badjao communities and are networking with local congregations who are planting churches among this unreached group. The area they live in is more wretched than most of the kids have ever seen, with one-room houses on stilts over a foul-smelling swamp, accessible only by planks with gaping holes between them, starting with three boards and ending with one only six inches wide. And there were no handrails! We prayed a lot for good balance and angelic help crossing the boards for the four trips there! The church was also on stilts, and the entire building swayed with the kids when they did our choreographed songs.

"We had an outdoor evangelistic meeting with many adults and extremely rowdy children. Pastor Jilun is doing a good job helping the people and has a Badjao congregation. He introduced us to the tribal chieftain, and we got to lay hands on him and pray, even though he is still not a Christian.

"On the first day of the Vacation Bible School in the packed church, there were some Badjao young women who said in English, 'We are Islam. Islam!' They came all three days and on the last day, with tears, confessed Jesus as Savior. Others, in tears, prayed lengthy, spontaneous prayers of faith in the Badjao language, known as Sama.

"For another VBS, we found a Badjao girl who spoke Cebuano/Visayan and had complex, three-level translation: our English speakers, a pastor to hear that and say it in Visayan, and the Badjao girl to hear Visayan and speak Badjao. It made such a huge impact there, having a large team come two years in a row (one asked where Kristin from last year's team was) and spend three days with them. The pastor's wife thanked me profusely for coming.

"The entire Badjao community knew we were there, and adults came to hear the gospel, watch the dramas and songs, and see us showing God's love to their kids. We used the wordless book approach, which symbolizes each step in explaining the gospel with a different color. On the first day the kids made the book as their craft. When we arrived on the second day, about a hundred Badjao kids were waiting outside the church waving their wordless books!"

the translator came up, Jodie asked him to find out what was wrong with the girl. The girl had leprosy. Jodie fought the urge to yank her hand away and run to wash it off. In 2003 we had shared the gospel at a leprosy community in Quito, Ecuador. This group of people suffered from the social stigma and rejection of the disease as well as the physical effects. Our teenage team couldn't help but love the people, hugging them and showing no fear of the disease. They had a powerful impact on the community. Leprosy is actually not very contagious and can be controlled by medicine now, but in ancient times it was a death sentence to be pronounced a leper.

So the four men with leprosy talked about their fate and one suggested, "Let's go to the enemy camp and beg for mercy. Maybe they'll feel sorry for us. What do we have to lose? We're dying of leprosy anyhow. We'll starve if we stay here—the worst they can do is kill us."

> And they rose at twilight to go to the camp of the Syrians; and when they had come to the outskirts of the Syrian camp, to their surprise no one was there. For the Lord had caused the army of the Syrians to hear the noise of chariots and the noise of horses—the noise of a great army; so they said to one another, "Look, the king of Israel has hired against us the kings of the Hittites and the kings of the Egyptians to attack us!" Therefore they arose and fled at twilight, and left the camp intact—their tents, their horses, and their donkeys—and they fled for their lives. And when these lepers came to the outskirts of the camp, they went into one tent and ate and drank, and carried from it silver and gold and clothing, and went and hid them; then they came back and entered another tent, and carried some from there also, and went and hid it. (2 Kings 7:5–8)

They hobbled up the road shouting, "Please have mercy on us! We're just four pitiful starving beggars. Please give us a bread crust! Let us dig through your dumpster!"

But no one responded. As they arrived at the Syrian army camp, they found an incredible sight—the place was empty. God had brought terror on the enemy soldiers, and they had run for the hills, leaving everything behind them. Four desperate men went looking for mercy and found the provision of God. They couldn't believe their good fortune. Just think of them running into the kitchen tent. The tables were piled high with food for the soldiers who had fled. To them it was Olive Garden, Golden Corral, Pizza Hut, and Red Lobster rolled into one—with Cheesecake Factory for dessert.

Then they saw the tents piled high with the treasures the Syrians had plundered from all the nations they had conquered. The poor beggars tried on the king's robes and jeweled crowns. "Hey, how do I look?"

Talk about a rags-to-riches story! Everything they needed was all around them. There was enough food to feed an army. They ate and ate. They were having a great time.

> Then they said to one another, "We are not doing right. This day is a day of good news, and we remain silent. If we wait until morning light, some punishment will come upon us. Now therefore, come, let us go and tell the king's household." (2 Kings 7:9)

One of them realized, "Wait a minute! We have more here than we could possibly eat, but back in the city people are starving."

Can you picture the contrast? Here they're wearing the king's clothes and barbecuing Syrian steaks.

Over there they're plotting murder and cannibalism and wondering what Grandma would taste like. The men realized their responsibility to share what God had given them. "Those are our neighbors back there. Our families. The people we've known all our lives, the people of our city—they're dying! We've got to tell them."

> So they went and called to the gatekeepers of the city, and told them, saying, "We went to the Syrian camp, and surprisingly no one was there, not a human sound—only horses and donkeys tied, and the tents intact." And the gatekeepers called out, and they told it to the king's household inside. (2 Kings 7:10–11)

They ran back and pounded on the gate. Well, maybe they just hobbled back and knocked with their remaining fingers. "Let us in! We have good news! God has defeated our enemies and provided for all our needs. There's all you can eat and more—free for the taking. You don't have to die. There's enough for everyone!"

> So the king arose in the night and said to his servants, "Let me now tell you what the Syrians have done to us. They know that we are hungry; therefore they have gone out of the camp to hide themselves in the field, saying, 'When they come out of the city, we shall catch them alive, and get into the city.'"
>
> And one of his servants answered and said, "Please, let several men take five of the remaining horses which are left in the city. Look, they may either become like all the multitude of Israel that are left in it; or indeed, I say, they may become like all the multitude of Israel left from those who are consumed; so let us send them and see." Therefore they took two chariots with horses; and the king sent them in the direction of the Syrian army, saying, "Go and see." And they went after them to the Jordan; and indeed all the road was full of garments and weapons which the Syrians had thrown away in their haste. So the messengers returned and told the king. Then the people went out and plundered the tents of the Syrians. (2 Kings 7:12–16)

Some of the people said, "Yeah, right! You must be working for the Syrians. You just want us to open the gate so the enemy can get inside."

But others looked through the peephole and said, "You know, those guys really look pretty healthy, for lepers. That one is still munching on a taco. Let's go see."

A few men went to check it out, and they found out it was all true. They rushed back to tell everyone. "It's true. It's true." The people stampeded from the city to feast on God's blessing.

A Parable of Our Lives

Remember I said this story is also a parable of our lives? You and I are the men with leprosy in this story. We were doomed with the incurable disease of our sin, and our lives were falling apart a little at a time. Can anyone say AMEN?

Maybe you were raised in a Christian family and met the Lord when you were very young, so you never had a long season of darkness and sin in your life. If that describes you, picture how your life might be different if you took away the Christian parents, Christian school, church, youth group, or the influence of godly relatives and friends. How lost could you be? What might your life be like now?

Maybe you weren't raised in a Christian environment, and you know all too well the negative impacts of being surrounded by a godless culture.

Whatever our history, most of us came to the end of ourselves at some point. We were desperate, empty people who knew there was nothing for us in the doomed city, so we went looking for mercy and found the provision of God.

God has defeated our enemy and given us so much. I'm not talking about things. The kingdom of God is not about Mercedes, money, and mansions. It's about righteousness, peace, and joy in the Holy Spirit. It's about access to God by faith in Christ, a clear conscience, and forgiveness of sins. It's about a Father who loves us.

We're like the lepers, coming out of a place of death into life. We have meaning and purpose in our lives now. But while we feast on God's blessings, the people of our city, of *every* city, are empty and

Basic health-care provider to people who rarely see a doctor. Preferably someone willing to study, work hard, and respond quickly to emergencies.

In the United States, most people are able to receive medical attention for even the smallest health problems. Yet in many countries, there are limited options for people to go to a hospital, as it might be too expensive, too far, or only open to select people. Minor ailments such as a small cut could become life threatening if the cut gets infected and a person can't afford antibiotics. Common colds and flu can be fatal to children without fever reducers such as ibuprofen or aspirin, and there is no help if someone's parent has a heart attack or stroke. Medical missionaries are needed around

the world, and even limited training can provide significant aid to a clinic, village, or city.

In the summer of 2000, eighteen-year-old Hilary Walker went on a King's Kids mission trip to the Philippines. She loved the people and culture and knew God was calling her to return. That September, Hilary moved to the Philippines and enrolled in a two-year midwifery school. Upon completion, she married David Overton, and they opened Glory Reborn, a free clinic for the poorest women in the city. Their vision was to bring quality care to women and children regardless of socioeconomic status. Nine years later, Glory Reborn has delivered three thousand babies, has a full-time staff of thirty Filipina nurses and midwives, two on-staff counselors, one social worker, seven health classes, and monthly parties to provide free vaccinations to countless children. Hilary attended medical school in the Philippines to become a doctor and even received an award from the president of the Philippines for her work.

Every week, Hilary and David volunteer medical aid in a red-light district and women's prison, and at one point they were asked by the mayor of Cebu to take over the

only public hospital on the island. Most importantly, Hilary and David have made an eternal impact on the nation of the Philippines, as they share the love of Jesus with every family who comes to the clinic through the gospel message, prayer, Bible studies, and baby dedications.

Are you interested in medicine? Prayerfully consider whether God has a purpose for your career in a Third World country. You might be the instrument God uses to bring hope, healing, and the gospel to a community that is in desperate need.

It's your world—do something today!

Local need: Call a local hospital and ask if you and two of your friends can visit the children's floor. Take card games and coloring books, and then at the end of your visit, ask to pray with the children.

International need: Join Glory Reborn's vision of Healthy Moms, Healthy Babies, and Hopeful Hearts by participating in the iSaved2Lives campaign. By donating just one dollar a day (either $30 a month or $365 a year), you can help ensure the health of a mother and her newborn. Go to *www.gloryreborn.com* to get involved today.

dying. Empty and desperate people will try to fill themselves up with something, anything, no matter how repulsive it is to us. We condemn and judge them because we've forgotten what life is like without Jesus. We've forgotten the hopelessness and the pain. The lost don't know of another way to fill the need that aches inside. Yes, their sins cry out for judgment, but God sees their need for Him.

Proverbs 27:7

_____

_____

Some people's stomachs are hungry, but others' souls are hungry. There is a gnawing emptiness of the soul that cries out to be filled. When people are ignorant of Jesus or have decided to reject Him, their emptiness seeks fulfillment in sin. Don't you see this around you every day?

While we're enjoying God's goodness, we need to do what the four men with leprosy did. This is a day of good news! The word *gospel* means good news. We can't keep the good news to ourselves. Yes, let's eat our fill from God's table and enjoy Him, but let's not forget the others! We have a responsibility to our hometown and to the ends of the earth, to let them know what Jesus has done. When Jesus said "Go" (Matthew 28:19), it was to all of us. Whether He sends you across the street or across the ocean is up to Him. Our message is that God has defeated the enemy and that every good thing is found in Jesus Christ.

What if the four men had said, "If the people in our city get hungry enough, they'll come looking and find what we found"? Or what if one said, "Let's go back," and the others said, "No, they're doing okay back there. It's not so bad. They like donkey heads and dove droppings and boiled children"? Or what if the lepers had delayed for a month, gorging on Syrian delicacies, and finally waddled back to the city? "What! You knew and didn't tell us? You had plenty while I watched my family die!" the people would cry out. "Well," the men might respond, "we didn't think you'd be interested. We didn't think you'd believe us."

Remember the Golden Rule? Do unto others as you would have them do unto you (Matthew 7:12)? If you were a starving person, you would want someone to tell you where to find food. You wouldn't want them to be laid back about it. You'd want them to grab you by both shoulders, look you in the eye, and say, "Look at me, trust me, believe me! It's all there. It's true!"

The Message of Jesus

Think about this: Over two thousand years a chain of events brought the gospel to you. It went from one country to the other to the next. Brave people crossed oceans and told our ancestors. People died carrying this message. Finally, the hope and peace came to you. The question is, will the gospel come to a dead end in our lives? Will it keep going or stop with us?

The responsibility belongs to each of us. There's a huge world full of people looking for something to fill their emptiness, and we know only Jesus can do that.

As I've traveled through twenty-five nations, I've been amazed at how much people are alike. It doesn't matter what color their skin is, what language they speak, or what kind of home they live in. They all have hopes and dreams and fears. They all want a happy life, something better for their children, and satisfaction inside. Where are they going to find it?

Haggai 2:7

_____

_____

Jesus is the Desire of Nations. He's the One people are looking for, even if they don't know it yet.

Psalm 107:9

_____

_____

Jesus is the only One who can offer satisfaction to hungry and longing souls.

Boldness for God

What is your part in God's plan to reach the lost? What is God saying to you? Some of you may be hearing His call to serve in your city or somewhere around the world. Don't let fear keep you back from the most exciting and fulfilling adventure you can ever have—the adventure of serving God. Some of you may need to pray for boldness to do what God has already prompted you to do—to reach out to that neighbor or coworker or classmate or friend or relative, that person you see every day who has a hungry soul.

Psalm 138:3

_____

_____

There's an important key in that verse. We tend to wait passively for God to give us things we're not sure we really want. Contrast this passivity with our persistence in seeking God when it's something we really want.

We realize that if we ask for boldness, God might actually hear us and give it to us. That would mean He expects us to use it, and that might be uncomfortable. That's why we wait for God to change us someday, maybe, if He gets around to it, rather than actively seeking Him for the things He makes clear are His will for us. We're buying time for our own desires.

The verse above says that when we cry out to God, He will answer us that same day. Crying out to God is drastically different from passively waiting. It's the difference between a prayer with passion and fervency and one that comes out with a yawn. Who's willing to say, "God, use me to reach a world full of perishing people"? Who's willing to cry out to God until He *is* using you to reach a world full of perishing people?

Romans 12:10–12

_____

_____

Take a step back and look at your life. Are you seeking fulfillment inside or outside of a relationship with God? God has offered Himself to you and invites you into the incredible adventure of serving Him. He will give you boldness you need if you cry out to Him. Jesus is calling you today!

WRAP-UP

Let's wrap this up and apply it to our lives. Let's put the illustration of the starving men with leprosy into a fresh prayer that sums up all we have seen so far.

Father, I'm like the men with leprosy—helpless apart from You. You've been so good to me. I realize how empty my life would be without Jesus, and I see so many empty lives around me. I've kept the Good News to myself for so long. I've let the fear of man control me, and I've just been selfish, thinking of myself and not caring about this lost world. Today I'm surrendering to You. O God, give me boldness and strength in my soul. Don't let me live a self-absorbed, self-centered life while the people around me live and die lost. Give me Your compassion for them. Help me to look beyond myself and see their needs. Mold my heart so it's like Yours. In Jesus' name. Amen.

What stands out to you in this prayer?

_____

_____

How will you put it into practice?

_____

_____

What has God been saying to you this week?

_____

_____

How does this affect your daily life?

_____

_____

How does this affect your life plans?

_____

_____

SCRIPTURE MEMORY

2 Peter 3:9
The Lord is not slack concerning His promise, as some count slackness, but is longsuffering toward us, not willing that any should perish but that all should come to repentance.

Matthew 6:32–33
For after all these things the Gentiles seek. For your heavenly Father knows that you need all these things. But seek first the kingdom of God and His righteousness, and all these things shall be added to you.

DAILY BIBLE READING

✓ Check when completed

Sunday	Ecclesiastes 1–6
Monday	Ecclesiastes 7–12
Tuesday	Song of Solomon 1–8
Wednesday	Isaiah 1–4
Thursday	Isaiah 5–8
Friday	Isaiah 9–12
Saturday	Isaiah 13–16

BIBLE READING QUESTIONS/THOUGHTS

_____
_____
_____
_____
_____
_____
_____
_____
_____
_____
_____

PRAYER NEEDS THIS WEEK

_____
_____
_____
_____
_____
_____
_____
_____
_____

3

Lesson three

LOST COINS

Do you ever look at coins and wonder about the people whose images are on them? If you have, you aren't alone. Jesus and His disciples talked about the images on coins. In fact, the Bible has a lot to say about coins. This chapter is all about coins—about the images on them, about their value, about God's pursuit of lost coins, and about how we spend our coins for the sake of other coins.

WHOSE IMAGE?

First, let's look at a simple illustration from God's Word that makes a profound point:

Then they asked Him, saying, "Teacher, we know that You say and teach rightly, and You do not show personal favoritism, but teach the way of God in truth: Is it lawful for us to pay taxes to Caesar or not?"

But He perceived their craftiness, and said to them, "Why do you test Me? Show Me a denarius. Whose image and inscription does it have?"

They answered and said, "Caesar's."

And He said to them, "Render therefore to Caesar the things that are Caesar's, and to God the things that are God's."

But they could not catch Him in His words in the presence of the people. And they marveled at His answer and kept silent. (Luke 20:21–26)

Ancient tradition said that all coins belonged to the one whose face was on them. In other words, Caesar owned all the coins bearing his picture. He let people use them, but they were still his property. Jesus said to give the coins back to Caesar. Then He spoke very pointedly for us to give ourselves to God, because God's image is on us.

Genesis 1:27

_____

_____

Coins were made by stamping a metal disk with a die. In Bible days there was a change of coins when a new ruler came into power, because the new ruler wanted his own image, not the face of the past ruler, on the coins. God uses the word _image_ over eighty times in the Bible to refer to idols. Here is one instance:

Deuteronomy 5:8

_____

_____

The Lord was against images because they represented allegiance to another god.

Isaiah 44:17

_____

_____

Since you were made in the image of God, God has a claim on your life. You belong to Him, and He is jealous for you. He wants everyone stamped with His image (and that's everyone on planet Earth) to be His. Just as with Caesar's coins, there is a mark of ownership on your life. Giving your life to anyone other than the One who put His image on you just wouldn't be right.

Jesus said to give to God whatever has His image on it—that means your heart and life. This includes your future, plans, talents, and abilities. Your time, energy, and thoughts. Your possessions, money, desires, career, education, and relationships. Your whole self. We're His property. We can't do whatever we want with our lives, because these are not our lives anymore—they are His.

Proverbs 23:26

_____

_____

Romans 14:7–9

_____

_____

Stamped with His Image

Is there a new ruler in your life since you gave your life back to the Lord? Your old life may not have looked much like Jesus' life, but if you belong to Him now, He is in the process of stamping a new image on you. You were stamped once with the image of your Creator and are being stamped again with the image of your Redeemer. You're His coin!

Romans 8:29

_____

_____

1 Corinthians 15:49

_____

_____

God is at work transforming your life, and His goal is plain: to remake you in the image of Jesus. He planned this from the beginning of eternity, and He won't quit until it's done.

Romans 12:1–2

_____

_____

Have you ever felt like a failure as a Christian? Like you're just not getting there, no matter how hard you try? There's hope! God promises to do the work of transformation, the restamping of His image. It's not about your effort; it's about His power. Read these promises and take heart.

Philippians 2:13

_____

_____

2 Corinthians 3:18

_____

_____

Romans 8:30

_____

_____

Philippians 1:6

_____

_____

LOST COINS

We've established that coins are people, symbolically speaking. Now let's look at a parable that Jesus tells about coins:

Luke 15:8–10

_____

_____

The woman in this parable symbolizes God looking for lost people. It's not enough for God to have some of His coins; He wants _all_ of His lost coins. Every person has value.

A coin may be worth far more than the actual value of a small piece of metal. It is worth whatever value is assigned to it, whatever the government tells us it's worth. In the same way, people are worth whatever God, who stamped them with His image, says they are worth, and He says His lost coins are worth actively searching for. When the woman saw one coin was missing, she couldn't be content without it. She couldn't rest but got out the flashlight, swept everywhere, moved furniture, looked under the couch cushions. She searched carefully and didn't give up until she found it.

If this was just a story about some woman who lost a quarter, we might think she's either really poor or really strange or really greedy. Unless the missing coin was gold or something, why make it such a big deal? But it's not just an earthly story; it's about God and the people who know His heart. It's about a yearning love, desperate to do everything possible so no one is left out. It's about God.

1 Timothy 2:4

_____

_____

2 Peter 3:9

_____

_____

_____

_____

SMALL CHANGE

You're walking down the street and out of the corner of your eye you see a coin on the ground. What does it take to get you to bend down and pick it up? You have to decide if it's worth the trouble. If it's a penny, maybe not. A dime? A quarter? Once a girl from King's Kids was raising money for a mission trip and saw a hundred-dollar bill blowing through the Sam's Club parking lot. You would probably stop to pick that up!

But what about people? Do you see some people as having more value than others? Are some more worth the effort to bend down and pick up?

Many times we are so preoccupied with our own lives that we don't even notice the people around us. We have our own worries, deadlines, stresses, crushes, plans, goals, and activities. Yet all around us there are God's lost coins. We notice them if they're somebodies—the popular, the beautiful, people worth something in this life—but do we notice the nobodies, the small change? God does.

True Story

We can't go by the world's value system to see what people are worth to God. Take the example of Antonio in Juárez, Mexico. He was a thirty-seven-year-old garbage picker who worked in the city dump before being paralyzed in an accident. Antonio was carried to us on a stretcher when we had an outreach to the handicapped. He was a quadriplegic, dependent on his elderly parents for everything—feeding, washing, bathroom use. I watched a Christian nurse from Texas spend two days tending to his bedsores, making him more comfortable, and teaching his parents how to take care of him. Why so much investment of time, effort, and money into Antonio? Because he's worth it to the Lord. Antonio was on the lowest rung of the status ladder. If he had been healed from paralysis, he would still have been an illiterate, unskilled garbage picker, but God saw something more in him. Antonio met Jesus that week and died a few years ago. God found one of His lost coins.

1 Corinthians 1:27–29

_____

_____

James 2:1–5

_____

_____

After thirty-two years of youth missions on every continent, I know the poor, and they are the same all over the world: simple people just trying to get by, to feed their kids, struggling every day of their lives. They are the type of people Jesus used to preach to: farmers and fishermen and shepherds. Most of them don't care much about politics. They are used to being trampled by the strong and have little hope for a better future. And they're precious to God, every single one. The most wretched glue-sniffing beggars we saw in Nicaragua, the poorest street children trying to pick our pockets in Mumbai, the desperate in Haiti, the kids who live like animals on the streets of major cities in South America—they're all made in the image of God, and each one is infinitely valuable to Him.

Bringing it closer to home, the people society thinks are nobodies are all somebody in God's eyes. That includes the homeless, the poor, the addicted, the outcast. It's the same with the nobodies around you every day at school or work. They too are valued lost coins.

As Christians we should show respect to everyone we encounter. When we eat in a restaurant, we shouldn't leave a mess for the busboy to clean up. He's made in the image of God. In the same way, we shouldn't make life harder for janitors by not cleaning up after ourselves. Those janitors are made in the image of God. We should especially show respect to our family members. We can so easily take our parents or siblings for granted. All people should receive our undivided attention when they talk to us. Be nice to people—even telemarketers!

Sometimes the image of God is so corrupted by sin that it's hard to believe it's still there. As Christians we need to learn that even if we find someone's lifestyle and sin completely repulsive, that person is God's coin. The Father needs to find the person and stamp the image of Jesus over that image of the devil in his or her life.

VALUE IN GOD'S EYES

Take a moment to read the True Story on the next page. Finished? Here's the big question: Which of those lost coins was worth more to the Lord? The answer is that they were worth the same amount. Jesus gave His life for both. Which one was worth more in the world's eyes? Obviously the young, successful stockbroker. But the yearning in the Father's heart to find both of these sons was the same.

Acts 10:34

_____

_____

Romans 10:11–13

_____

_____

We are a nation prone to arrogance—the feeling that my coin is worth more than your coin. The flip side to this arrogance is a sense of having no value at all.

The Hindus have a greeting we learned during a two-month outreach in India: *Namaste.* I discovered this means "I bow to the divinity within you." As with all of Satan's deceptions, Hinduism has a little truth mixed in with its lies. There is no divinity within people unless they have Jesus living in their hearts. But the truth mixed in is this: We are all made in God's image. Every person should be treated with respect and honor as the creation of God. In this way we honor Him.

We saw the power of this while ministering in the Philippines for four summers. These are precious people we have grown to love, and we hope to return there. The Philippines is a nation of ninety-five million people who often display a deep-rooted sense of worthlessness. So many people we met had a sense of inferiority. Many Filipinos are not very tall, and it bothers them. The Philippines is a nation trying to find its worth in education, technology, and materialism. We were there showing people that their worth comes from the fact that God loves them enough to send His Son to die for them and rescue them from the consequences of their sins.

The Filipino kids would come to our American kids, saying, "Oh, you have such beautiful white skin." Our kids would say, "You have such beautiful dark skin." They would compare their smaller noses and straight, black hair to larger American noses and variety of hair types. It was sad and shocking to us to see booths in their stores advertising skin-lightening creams for sale. The Filipino kids were shocked to find out Americans pay good money to tanning salons to get darker skin. Americans sometimes give lots of money to plastic surgeons to get smaller noses. People with straight hair curl it, and those with curly hair straighten it. Nobody is happy.

The image of God looks one way in Africa, another way in Japan, and other ways in Mexico and Norway and Syria. Of course, the image of God is much more than skin deep. It's the eternal nature of human beings, the only part of creation given a soul. It's the mind, will, and emotions, the capacity

True Story

I was on a plane coming back from New York. When I fly, I always see if God is setting up an opportunity to talk to the person sitting next to me about Him. Sometimes people are totally disinterested. If you pull out your Bible and they suddenly act like they are asleep, this is a good indication they aren't open. But sometimes they are sitting next to you because the Lord has set up a divine appointment. I've met other missionaries, witnessed to Muslims, talked to a New Age woman who practiced goddess worship, shared the gospel with a Chinese computer programmer, and so on.

On this flight the young man sitting next to me was reading about the stock market. I wanted to start up a conversation, so I told him that I didn't know much about stocks and asked him if he did. He was a stockbroker just a few years out of college and already making $200,000 a year. Bill was talkative, handsome, and friendly. He told me the best-paid men in his office were making $7.5 million a year. He had a bright future and was engaged to a TV anchor. Bill had it all . . . in the world's eyes.

As the conversation progressed, Bill asked me what I did. He was fascinated by stories of our ministry around the world, and I presented the message of Jesus to him. Bill got very serious and said the only time in his life when he really felt good about himself was in college, when he went on a Peace Corps type of service project one summer and helped the poor. He seemed envious that I did that kind of thing all the time and started to tell me how his life was empty. He said even his fiancée didn't really bring him fulfillment, because she was so materialistic and worldly. When the plane landed, Bill was thinking seriously about God's claim on his life and what really matters.

I was pumped! Getting on the next flight, I was ready to minister to the next person sitting by me. As I walked down the aisle looking for my row, I noticed a very strange woman sitting in seat A. Mine was seat B. The woman's head was bowed down, with long hair covering her face. As I sat down and offered her a magazine, she wouldn't look up or talk to me. Occasional glimpses of the face behind the hair confirmed my suspicions. This wasn't a woman. It was a young transvestite man—in pantyhose and high heels.

I admit that it was hard to see this person as someone stamped with the image of God. But I realized this could be another divine appointment. The young man slowly began to relax, and I found out he was going to a friend's funeral. I had a guess about why the friend had died. When I told him a little about myself, he started to pour out a story of pain—an abusive father, divorced parents, and a life without God. I tried to share the hope found in Jesus, but his heart was completely closed. I watched him as he left the plane, still broken and empty, still a lost coin.

Compassionate servant to give love, affection, and time to orphans and street children. Must be willing to play games, care for needs, and act as a mother or father figure to displaced youth.

Children become orphans for many reasons. Many thousands are orphans because their parents are killed by disease, war, and natural disasters. Other children are functionally orphans because their family cannot afford to feed them and are therefore rejected and sent to live on the streets. Some children are orphans because their parents turn to alcohol, drugs, crime, or prostitution, and they are abandoned so the parents can pursue their addictions. Some children are abandoned merely because they are girls. In 2004, there were an estimated 143 million orphans around the world.

- In 2003, there were roughly 35 million orphans in India alone.
- It is estimated that the numbers of orphans will grow by 16 million to 20 million a year.
- In Texas, there are 13,111 children waiting to be adopted.

Once a child is orphaned in a developing country, she must fight daily to survive. Most are immediately put on the street and have to find a way to make money so they can eat and have shelter. Can you imagine making these decisions as a six-year-old? These children

are the most vulnerable part of society and are preyed upon by stronger, corrupt individuals. Many orphans become victims of trafficking, whether it be through slavery, prostitution, or drugs. Some are kidnapped and forced to become child soldiers. Others die because of disease, starvation, or lack of shelter, and many turn to substance abuse to cope with their circumstances.

God cares deeply about orphans. He speaks about them repeatedly in the Bible, and as the Good Father, His heart breaks over their plight. God sees every single abandoned child. He intimately knows his heartache, his daily fight to survive, and the ease with which he falls into great danger. When we read statistics about orphans, we might see huge numbers; however, God mourns over each forsaken and forgotten child. He commands the church to plead justice on their behalf and provide for their needs. We can respond to His cry today.

In 2004, our King's Kids team went to Ethiopia, where there are sixty thousand to one hundred thousand street people in the capital alone. While there, we worked with a great ministry called Win Soul, which was started in 1997 by a group of Ethiopian teenagers. These Christian youth saw the desperate needs in their nation and began a ministry to provide for street people. Since then, they have ministered to over fifteen thousand homeless in their city. Daily, they give Bible teaching and food to 120 people, enroll countless children in their elementary schools, have helped 130 people begin their own businesses, developed a sponsorship program for orphans, and have an HIV/AIDS prevention program. It is amazing to look at the lives of Christians who live beyond their own needs and comfort. Be inspired by the faithful work of

those in Ethiopia who have forever changed the lives and eternities of thousands in their nation!

It's your world—do something today!

Volunteer with your city's Preparation for Adult Living (PAL) program or a similar one. This monthly program works to equip teenagers who are aging out of the foster care system for daily life on their own. Without families, many of them have no one to help them walk through serious challenges: getting a job, paying bills, filing tax forms, etc. Also, foster children rarely have a home to go to for Christmas, Thanksgiving, or other holidays. Connect and show support to a child in foster care, and you will be demonstrating the love of Jesus to a teenager who might not have anyone else. Go to *www.childwelfare.gov/outofhome/independent/* or *www.nrcyd.ou.edu/state-pages* to locate programs in your area.

Ask your pastor if your church can partner with WorldOrphan, an amazing Christian organization that connects Western churches to churches overseas in an effort to care for orphans. The Western church provides resources, mission trip opportunities, and communication to the foreign church and financially enables families in the foreign church to house, educate, and provide a family setting for orphans in the city. See *www.worldorphans.org* for more information.

Support a child's education through WinSoul ministries in Ethiopia. Just $150 a year will provide the funds for classes, healthy meals, Bible teachings, and community for children who are AIDS orphans, slaves, and very poor. Go to *www.wsg-street.org* to change a child's life today.

to know our Creator and to think what He thinks and feel what He feels. What do you think the Lord thinks about prejudiced people who despise others made in His image?

Galatians 3:28

_____

_____

Saving and Spending

Every coin has value. Our lives in Jesus have worth. What do you do with coins? You save them until you need something. Many of us have already spent the coin of our lives that belongs to God in many ungodly ways. Many of us wasted a lot of years before we realized the Lord's claim on our lives.

1 Peter 4:3

_____

_____

God is a wise businessman. He doesn't waste His coins. First He *saves* us, and then He *spends* us. And how does God spend us? On others! The apostle Paul knew how this works and described how his life was spent.

2 Corinthians 12:15

_____

_____

God wants to spend us, even on those who won't appreciate or love us back. We can only love without being loved back when we are rooted in God. Then we can see life in the light of eternity and not think about ourselves so much. Maybe it would be more accurate to say that God wants to invest us—to use one coin to gain more coins. Remember how pleased He was with the men in the parable who used their coins to get more?

Matthew 25:20–23

_____

_____

We can give God our lives only if we trust Him not to waste our lives and if we count His plans and purposes as being greater than our own. We can look forward to being spent only when we really know His heart and the value He places on His lost coins.

Pursuing the Wrong Kind of Coins

Many Christians are pursuing the wrong kind of coins—the ones with the image of Caesar instead of the ones with the image of God. Our priorities in life have gotten confused. We're pursuing what's valuable to the world instead of what's valuable to God.

Matthew 6:32–33

_____

_____

Luke 16:13–15

_____

_____

We've forgotten that Jesus said to give those coins back to Caesar. In other words, they aren't all that important. We're to keep a light touch on things of this world, not a clenched grip.

1 Timothy 6:6–11

_____

_____

This message is a call to value what God values. It's a call to see people through the Father's eyes, to help God search for His lost coins. It's a call to see the worth of every person, no matter how insignificant that person may be in the world's eyes. For some, it may be a call to give up the small and selfish pursuits in life and let God invest your coin. What could He do if we were fully surrendered to Him? How much of a return could the Lord get from our lives? Which kind of coins are most valuable to you? Are you pursuing coins with the image of Caesar on them or coins with the image of God on them?

WRAP-UP

Let's wrap this up and apply it to our own lives. Let's put the illustration of lost coins into a fresh prayer that sums up all we have seen this week.

Father, I've valued people based on the world's view of them, not Yours. Let me know Your heart. Let me see people through Your eyes. I have ignored the small change, and I've been too busy to pick up lost coins that didn't seem worth the effort. Help me to value them as You do.

Lord, I'm so selfish. I want what I want, right now. I think of myself first. I realize that You have the right to claim my life as Your own possession. Help me to live this out. Help me not to pull back into selfishness when You have something for me to do.

Spend me, Lord. Make my life count. I don't want to get to heaven and suddenly realize I've wasted the only life I'll ever have on earth. I don't want to miss the plan You created me to fulfill. Let my life affect people around me for Your glory. And let me find some of Your lost coins this week. In Jesus' name. Amen.

What stands out to you in this prayer?

_____

_____

How will you put it into practice?

_____

_____

What has God been saying to you this week?

_____

_____

How does this affect your daily life?

_____

_____

How does this affect your life plans?

_____

_____

SCRIPTURE MEMORY

Psalm 82:3–4
Defend the poor and
   fatherless;
Do justice to the afflicted and
   needy.
Deliver the poor and needy;
Free them from the hand of
   the wicked.

James 1:27
Pure and undefiled religion
before God and the Father is
this: to visit orphans and widows in their trouble, and to
keep oneself unspotted from
the world.

COMPLETE THE MISSION REPORT ON THE NEXT PAGE.

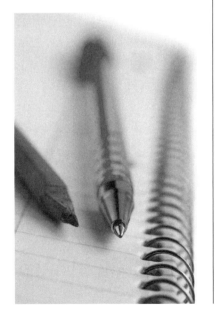

DAILY BIBLE READING

✓ Check when completed	
Sunday	Isaiah 17–20
Monday	Isaiah 21–23
Tuesday	Isaiah 24–27
Wednesday	Isaiah 28–30
Thursday	Isaiah 31–35
Friday	Isaiah 36–39
Saturday	Isaiah 40–43

BIBLE READING QUESTIONS/THOUGHTS

_____
_____
_____
_____
_____
_____
_____
_____
_____
_____
_____

PRAYER NEEDS THIS WEEK

_____
_____
_____
_____
_____
_____
_____
_____

4

MISSION REPORT

We recommend using *Operation World* (7th edition) by Jason Mandryk as a reference. See page 12 for details.

Country name:

Capital:

Population:

Ethnic groups:

Official language(s):

Literacy rate:

Average income (or GDP per capita):

Major religions:

Percentage of evangelical Christians:

Number of missionaries to the country:

Prayer needs:

1.

2.

3.

4.

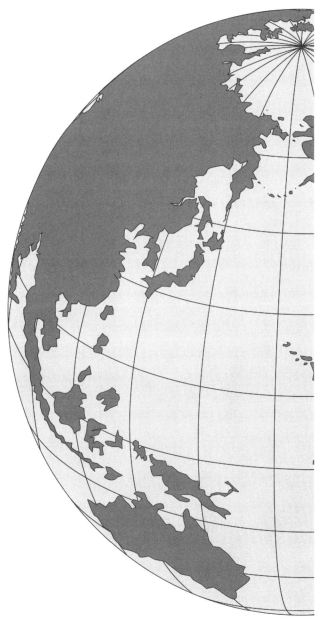

Lesson *four*

REMEMBER THE POOR

Have you noticed how many times the Bible talks about those who are weak and in need of extra care and consideration from others? Here is a list of people to whom God pays special attention:

- widows
- orphans
- the poor
- the needy
- the oppressed

- strangers
- foreigners
- aliens
- the fatherless
- the lame and sick

Malachi 3:5

_____

_____

Galatians 2:10

_____

_____

This lesson will be a little different from the others, and I hope to communicate a particular burden of my heart. I'm going to intersperse Scripture with stories from our adventures with God all over the world. There won't be any True Story boxes, but all these stories are true. Let them sink into your heart, and listen for God's voice.

A FATHER IN NEED

"Help me, help me!" the shabbily dressed Mexican man's voice rang out in Spanish near the busy street corner in Los Mochis near the Pacific coast of Mexico. No one paid any attention, but I heard the

desperation and then saw it in the man's eyes as he looked all around him. He was a small man of Native American background, and he held a feverish young girl who was obviously very ill. Our mission team surrounded him and asked what was wrong. With a quavering voice he explained that his little girl was very sick, and he had pulled together enough money to bring her from his village to the city to see a doctor. His trembling hand pressed a crumpled slip of paper into mine as he explained that he had no money left to fill the prescription the doctor had given him. He didn't want anything else.

I'm aware of scams in many forms, deceptive beggars, and lies, but this appeal was truthful. I took the paper and told the man we would pay for the medicine. I had no idea how much it might cost or what made the little girl so sick, but our mission team was going to help this man no matter what. The team gathered around him as I went into the pharmacy. The clerk took the paper and returned with a box. I braced myself for the bill as I reached into the team money bag.

It was $1.57. I was floored as I realized that when my kids got sick, we had the best medical care, insurance, and hospitals nearby, and I have never had to beg in the streets for $1.57.

All this happened quickly, and when I returned, the team was praying for the weeping man. A crowd had gathered to see why all these gringos were surrounding one *indígena* and a sick little girl. It all came together in my mind, and I turned to our missionary friend and said, "Dan, *preach!*"

Dan stood on some steps near the pharmacy in this Mexican city and proclaimed the love of Jesus to the curious crowd. I thought, *This is the kingdom of God!*

Isaiah 61:1

_____

_____

Proverbs 14:21

_____

_____

Surviving Homelessness

Every mission trip has a defining moment when it becomes clear that the Lord has a life lesson for us to learn. In Russia it happened one afternoon in Yekaterinburg, which has over two million people and zero homeless shelters. We worked with the largest Pentecostal church in the area. On

Fridays the city's homeless youth come to the church for a free lunch and ministry time. They were such a pathetic group, ragged and unkempt. Some may have been released from orphanages, and others may have been runaways or kids forced to leave home.

Russian orphanages release kids to the streets at age eighteen, and these kids are unprepared to face life outside. Put yourself in their shoes for a minute. You're eighteen years old, and the only family you've ever known is within the walls of the orphanage. Maybe your drug-addicted mother gave you up at birth, or the government took you away from your abusive, alcoholic father. You might have faced repeated sexual abuse or violence, like the Russian orphan girl who lived with our family for three years and once said, "You learn not to cry, because then they just beat you more."

Now that you're at the age to be released from the orphanage, you have a tearful goodbye, gather your few possessions in a bag, and leave. When the door locks behind you, you're terrified. A man gets out of a car parked across the street and saunters over. "Where are you going to stay tonight?" he asks. "How are you going to eat?"

You have no idea what to do, but he offers to take you somewhere. The pimps always wait outside, like wolves waiting to prey on the weak. You get in the car. You have just entered the grim world of human trafficking. Soon you will face degradation beyond your worst nightmares, probably including drug addiction and an early death. It's very much like the movie *Taken,* which you may have seen.

The homeless kids in Yekaterinburg were not among the many who are bought and sold like cattle, but their lives were desperate nonetheless. Understanding that their lifestyle usually includes drug addiction, prostitution, and having no family was heartbreaking. The homeless live underground like rats—and with rats—in the tunnels beside the steam pipes during the long Russian winters, when they tell us snow reaches up to one's armpits.

We presented the gospel through testimonies and drama, fed them lunch, and even had a game of soccer, which they won easily. I felt compassionate as usual but somehow disconnected from them until all the official events were over and the Russian kids were hanging around. It was clear that they looked forward to these Friday lunches as an escape from the grim and difficult lives they had the rest of the week. The lunch was a chance to connect with their friends. I watched them laughing and joking, flirting and letting down their guard. They were just kids, much like our team kids. For a few hours on Friday, it didn't matter that they had to do degrading or shameful or evil or violent things to make money to survive each day. They didn't have all the stresses of fending for themselves, trying to be adults when they were really just teenagers, wondering what would happen tomorrow, avoiding the multitudes of dangers that homeless kids must face. At the church on Fridays, they could relax. My prayer for them is that they may come to know the Friend who will stick closer than a brother (Proverbs 18:24).

James 1:27

_____

_____

Isaiah 25:4

_____

_____

Jeremiah 22:15–16

_____

_____

The Man in the Front Row

The homeless Ethiopian men packed the church when word got out about a free meal. There were hundreds of them, and our team scrambled to serve the hot *injera* bread and traditional gravy-like topping. A surprising number of homeless people in Ethiopia are Christians, thrown out of their homes by Muslim family members who are angry about their conversion to Christ. The aroma in the room was strong, and not just because of the meal.

As I watched out for the safety of the kids in an unpredictable situation, a man in the front row stood out. He listened to the pastor preach in Amharic, and his mismatched shoes seemed to be a perfect example of a life pieced together, made to work, facing one obstacle after another. One sandal may have come from the dumpsters that are the normal source of food for homeless Ethiopians, and maybe the other was found by the side of the road. Somehow he had found a left one and a right one. Somehow they were roughly the right size. Life on the streets in Ethiopia moved forward.

Empathetic helper to understand hardships placed on homeless individuals and families. Must listen to stories, buy meals, and direct homeless families to shelters, jobs, and opportunities to regain control of their lives.

People become homeless for numerous reasons. Usually, someone will lose his job and is then unable to pay rent. Sometimes that person can live with family members or friends while he looks for a new job, but many times a person is forced to live out of her car or some other makeshift home. Without a home, shower, and clean clothes, it is harder for a person to find a new job. Her car might be taken away from her in the process, and all her remaining money goes toward food. This situation causes most people to feel totally hopeless! As a result, homeless people often turn to substances for comfort, and within a short time they lose control of their lives. For some homeless people, substance abuse might come at the beginning of their downward spiral.

- On any given night, there are over 600,000 homeless people in the United States.
- Around 50,000 of these homeless are youth.
- Nearly one million youth are homeless one night a year.
- One person who works full-time and makes minimum wage is unable to afford a two-bedroom apartment in most places in the United States.

In developing countries, homelessness is much different, as millions are born onto the streets and raised without a home. However, the sorrows of homelessness are no less difficult: homeless families usually beg for food, suffer tremendously from disease, and are victims of crime. Many street people rely on cheap fixes, such as sniffing glue, to ease their hunger pains, and most of them never receive any education. Homelessness is therefore a repeating cycle through generations and overlaps with numerous other tragic world issues.

When Leah Pryor was fourteen years old, she felt sad that her siblings would not be able to come home to visit for Christmas. This caused her to notice many homeless people in her city, and she recognized that most of them would not have any family during the holiday. She decided to bake cookies and make Christmas cards for the homeless, and in the weeks leading up to Christmas, she distributed them around the city.

The next year, homeless people continued to burn on her heart. She chose to do something about it and made care packages for them, including blankets, food, and hygiene products. She asked people from her church to join her efforts and then kept all the bags of goods in her parents' car. Whenever she gave out a bag, she also asked to pray for the person. At one point, Leah met some homeless brothers and a young couple who were living behind a Starbucks. She made friends with the woman, who cried at Leah's offer to help. Later, Leah learned that the woman had passed away, but Leah was confident that her time and prayers for the woman played a role in that woman accepting Jesus as Savior. Through a King's Kids outreach that included youth participants from several states, Leah helped her dad lead a weeklong program for the homeless.

This year, Leah hopes to turn her work into an ongoing ministry by asking other people to join her frequently in engaging the homeless.

It's your world—do something today!

Just like Leah, make care packages for homeless people in your city and keep them in your car so you can distribute them whenever you see a homeless person. Fill them with granola bars, bottled water, hygiene products, and a personal note that shares the gospel.

Matthew 25:35

_____

_____

Proverbs 22:9

_____

_____

Proverbs 28:27

_____

_____

THE PLIGHT OF THE LOWEST

The Tarahumara Indian people, who live in the rugged Sierra Madre of northwestern Mexico, are hard to reach. A primitive tribe of people who worship the idols of their ancestors, the Tarahumara believe that God made the Indians while the devil made everyone else. Many of them live in caves in the mountains, but some have migrated to towns and cities. Their average lifespan is only forty-five years.

We were working in poor areas in Mexico, going house to house with small bags of groceries and a Spanish Bible for each family, inviting them to evangelistic meetings we were holding after the searing sun went down. One afternoon we saw a Tarahumara mom carrying her young child in a papoose on her back. Far from her native home, she was digging in the trash can outside a produce market, hoping its discarded fruits and vegetables weren't too wilted and moldy. We stopped the van full of kids across the street and watched her for a while. Then we sent just one of the team, Veronica, the smallest and least threatening girl who spoke Spanish, to take her a bag of groceries. After all, if you were a Tarahumara mom, would you want a mob of Satan's people to surround you?

The woman immediately burst into tears, and our hearts broke for her. Tarahumaras are the lowest level in Mexican society, frequently earning half as much as other Mexicans for the same jobs. They are mostly uneducated and illiterate and are often sick. Most of all, they are lost without Jesus. As the woman cried, she allowed Veronica to hug her and talk with her. What an opportunity, to be allowed so close! Tonight there would be a feast in that family's little home.

I was walking in the same town near the train tracks when I spotted a much older Tarahumara woman on the ground under the train. Thinking she was hurt, I ran over, but stopped to witness an unusual sight. A heavy truck was backed up perpendicular to the open door of the train car, and Mexican men were loading 50-kilo (110-lb.) burlap bags of beans onto the train. Occasionally a bag had a tear and a few beans would fall out. The Tarahumara woman lay patiently, hoping for a bag to be snagged on the train door to provide her with a real bounty. She picked up the spilled beans, one at a time, gathering dinner.

Psalm 41:1

_____

_____

Proverbs 21:13

_____

_____

Stuck in Karma

In the mornings, the people who live on the streets in Kolkata, India, do some of the same things we do. They stretch, use the bathroom, make breakfast, bathe, get dressed, and head to work. That's where the similarities stop. The bathroom is usually a vacant lot and sometimes just the gutter of the

street. Showers are community gatherings at a water pump, like a fire hydrant, which gushes into the street. All the men and boys go together, laughing and talking, stripped to the waist; and at other times and places the girls and women wash up while completely dressed in elegant, if tattered, brightly colored saris. All of life takes place on the street, though cover during the monsoons is a must. Men with stools and scissors give haircuts, and vendors sell their wares.

Home for many is a particular stretch of sidewalk, as it was for some families we saw near the railway station. They kept just enough firewood to cook their rice, had little hope of privacy, and had even less hope of changing their lot in life. These people's parents or grandparents were likely raised in similar circumstances or in villages so poor that they decided to try their luck in the city. But jobs are scarce, and hope is squelched by the Hindu law of karma, which teaches them that they have earned their sufferings and must simply endure them. For many day laborers, work today might be unloading a truck, tomorrow painting a wall, and the day after digging for a construction project—and in India, women do construction right alongside the men, carrying heavy baskets of rocks on their heads, moving slowly but with determination. At least it puts rice on the table, if they have a table.

Where my family lived for a time, five hundred miles west of Kolkata, the plight of people around us was no better. Our neighbors lived in a patched-together tent with about four children. The family who lived next to them couldn't even afford a tent. They got up each morning and rolled up their meager possessions, placing them under the awning of an abandoned building while they searched for work. A few blankets, a water jug, some battered pots—that's all they owned. No one tried to steal what little they had. It would be bad for their karma.

1 Timothy 6:17–19

_____

_____

Proverbs 29:7

_____

_____

A Destitute Country

About a hundred children and teenagers in northern Haiti came together for a youth camp in the mountains. The Christian leaders who advertised and organized it kept lowering the price to help more

Feeder of the hungry, with eyes wide open to the plight of the starving. Must be willing to actively donate finances, volunteer in soup kitchens, and seek God's solutions for people unable to feed their families.

Think about the last time you were very hungry. Most likely, food became the most prominent thought in your mind, forcing you to stop whatever you were doing to eat. It might have made you irritable or emotional, and if you were at work, it probably hindered your performance. Now imagine that you were not able to find food and there were no grocery stores, no crops, and no food rations. What would you do?

For close to a billion people, hunger is more than a stomach growling between meals. Rather, it is a disabling struggle that perpetuates disease, prohibits daily functioning, and is life-threatening to parents, children, and friends. People with debilitating hunger

sometimes resort to dangerous means to provide for their families, and so hunger acts as fuel for civil unrest, crime, and the sex trade. It also poses the greatest threat to people who are already in a vulnerable situation: young children and the elderly. While there are enough resources on earth to feed the world's population, statistics show the following:

- Hunger affects 925 million people, only 2 percent of whom live in developed countries.
- Six countries (Ethiopia, Pakistan, India, the Democratic Republic of the Congo, Bangladesh, and Indonesia) contain 65 percent of the world's hungry people.
- 1.9 billion people suffer from iodine deficiency, which is the leading cause of brain damage and mental retardation. By adding iodine to table salt, this tragedy could be avoided.
- Five million children under five years old die each year from hunger.
- Hunger is the number one health risk in the world. It causes more economic, social, and bodily damage than tuberculosis, AIDS, and malaria combined.
- Hunger is brought on by natural disasters, drought, crime, war, and corrupt governments who use it as a way to control or punish their people.

God cares about the hungry. In the Bible, He repeatedly commands

us to feed the poor, and while Jesus was on earth, He actively responded to this plea. In fact, there were a few times when Jesus did not send people away from Him unless they had something to eat. He coupled spiritual food with tangible food, and by the frequency of His messages about the poor and hungry, we can know that He asks us to do the same. As we serve God, hunger should become an issue on our minds. Today, you can be part of the solution to this emergency.

It's your world—do something today!

Get involved locally: Volunteer in soup kitchens, homeless shelters, and women's shelters. If you know a particular person or family who is struggling financially, save up money and take them shopping. Get your church involved to do a grocery store gift card drive and give the cards out to people struggling in your congregation.

Get involved internationally: Feed a child every day for only $15 a month through Charlie's Lunch, a Christian organization that provides food for countless children in six countries. Go to *www.charlieslunch.com* for more information. Additionally, donate to Hope Enterprises, the only soup kitchen in Ethiopia. It has served seventy-eight thousand people a hot meal and also provides vocational training and messages on faith and hope. Go to *www.hopeenterprises.org* today.

attend, but still the minimal fee of five dollars was beyond many families' means, so we raised the funds and paid for them. The youth were so excited for a chance to get out of Gonaïves, the city where we

were staying. They loved the cooler mountain air, the mango trees, and the cool stream that flowed through the camp—which was also where we bathed. Conditions were a lot rougher than at any of the hundreds of camps I've led in the US, but we had a great time. Despite the complete lack of sports equipment or toys, the children played jacks by throwing a rock up in the air, scrambling to pick up smaller rocks, and catching the bigger one on the way down. The teenagers had traditional games, including a chant that grew faster and faster as they ran in a circle and collapsed in laughter. The language barrier wasn't much of a problem except for Bible study, and they worshipped with all their hearts.

Mealtimes were what impressed me most. Several women in a small hut cooked delicious chicken-and-rice dishes over an open fire. There was no refrigeration or any way to wash dishes adequately, so I prayed a lot. When the kids lined up for each meal, they received enormous portions of the savory food. Unlike at all the Western camps, where kids frequently turn up their noses at the food and throw away nearly full plates, the Haitian children, all the way down to the six-year-olds, ate every last bite. At the end of the meals there was nothing to clean off the plates except an occasional grain of rice. I had no idea how they could eat so much—the portions were too big for me! Little brown stomachs bulged with each breakfast and dinner.

The camp leaders shed more light on what was happening. The kids' perspective was this: there's food today, but there may not be any tomorrow or the next day, so eat all you can while it's available. The depth of this simple fact left me speechless. I've never known hunger, except when fasting or between meals, and there has always been a well-stocked refrigerator nearby or money in my pocket to buy something to eat. When I've prayed, "Give us this day our daily bread," it has been more symbolic than desperate.

Realizing the huge gap between my experiences and theirs, I asked the leaders, "When you were growing up, did you know hunger?" They looked back and forth into each other's eyes, silently, before answering the foolish white foreigner's question with a simple yes from one of the group. I was immediately humbled and silenced. They hadn't wanted to embarrass me by saying the sort of sarcastic remark that someone in our culture would have used: "Are you kidding? This is Haiti! Of course we were hungry. All the time! Hello!"

Haiti has left an imprint on my heart. I remember seeing Haitian men who have never worn shoes, their feet splayed out and wider than any you've ever seen from a life of heavy manual labor without shoes to support their feet. I still picture the teenage boy who confronted me just outside the airport during my first trip there. "Give me yo' shoes, mon! I no have no shoes!" he said. I was rattled and wondered whether I should give him the pair right off my feet, but I had brought only one pair and it would have looked rather strange if I preached at a national pastors' conference without shoes.

Poverty is a fact of life in Haiti, which was desperate and poor even before Tropical Storm Jeanne, in 2004, swept an estimated three thousand people from Gonaïves into the ocean with flash floods roaring down the mountainside and walls of brown water ten feet high scouring the streets. Haitians' lives were hard before the 7.0 earthquake devastated their capital in 2010 and put thousands into makeshift tent cities, where a cholera epidemic silently picked off 6,600 victims and infected nearly a quarter of a million others. Haitians are always awaiting the next blow in their ongoing fight to survive.

Proverbs 31:9

_____

_____

Proverbs 14:31

_____

_____

THE TEST BEFORE US

Why would I take a whole chapter to tell stories about poverty? Because God sees the poor as a priority and a test for His people. He could easily send manna from heaven for them, change the weather so they never shivered or were drenched in the rain, provide everything they needed—but He doesn't do it that way. Instead, He provides abundantly for His people and gives us a responsibility to help others. It's a test of whether we will selfishly keep the resources for ourselves or look out for others. It's a chance to express His heart and model His character, but many of us fail this test.

One last story. I've always loved the snow, winter sports, and skiing. Moving to the hot, dry desert of Texas from Alaska at age fifteen was a dramatic change. Occasionally it snows here, and kids rejoice at the chance to build a sandy snowman or throw a few snowballs, but even without snow we do have some very cold winter days. I can see the vast, poor city of Juárez, Mexico, from my backyard. I've been in many of the cardboard huts there over the years and watched children dig in the dump for food. I know how hard life can be there. Years ago, it was snowing one night, and I stopped thinking about how my kids would have fun taking a day off from school. Instead, I thought of the poor people just a dozen miles away in Mexico, who would be huddled together as wintry winds whipped through the gaps in the cardboard. Snow on their patched-together roofs would trickle through in icy drops. This realization ruined the beauty of the snow that night.

I clearly remember praying a prayer and hearing God's response to it. "Father, it's so cold outside. Lord, remember the poor. Do something and help them." As sure as I'm sitting at the keyboard right now, God immediately spoke back to me in my heart. "Vinnie, it's so cold outside. Vinnie, remember the poor. Do something and help them."

And we have. From vanloads of toys and blankets collected at Christmas to truckloads of food, to construction projects and new roofs, to several thousand American kids who have gone to Juárez to see sights firsthand that will change their lives forever—we have.

But hear this point: It's not enough to give a blanket or some food or fix a roof. Those are all necessary but temporary fixes. People are eternal, and genuine help will always touch them in an eternal way. We give in Jesus' name, using every practical means as a springboard to tell of His love, His sacrifice for their sins on the cross, His desire to take them from this world of suffering to an eternal home in heaven. The "social gospel" that brings no gospel at all misses the tremendous opportunity of joining practical help with spiritual help, touching the inner person instead of simply meeting the body's needs. We don't want to make the mistake of doing good deeds, feeling good about ourselves, and leaving a poor person warm and fed but with an empty soul and without a relationship with his or her Creator. Always, always, always care for the poor with a view toward their eternal souls.

Even as I wrote this chapter, I choked up remembering these life-changing situations. To you, these were just stories on paper. But not to me! I looked into those eyes, touched the people, heard their voices, and ate with them. My prayer is that you will read these stories and feel them inside, hear the call from Scripture, and be moved in your heart to do something for the people around the world who are in great need.

Wrap-up

Let's apply this to our lives and put it into a fresh prayer that sums up all we have seen this week.

Father, I usually just care about myself and a small circle of people who are close to me. Help me to learn your heart for a great big world of sorrow and suffering and need and pain. Help me to care about the poor as You do, seeing not only statistics but individuals who are precious to You, with needs that I can meet through Your provision in my life and Your love in my heart. Let me represent You to a world that needs You so very much. In Jesus' name. Amen.

What stands out to you in this prayer?

_____

_____

How will you put it into practice?

_____

_____

What has God been saying to you this week?

_____

_____

How does this affect your daily life?

_____

_____

How does this affect your life plans?

_____

_____

Scripture Memory

Matthew 9:36
But when He saw the multitudes, He was moved with compassion for them, because they were weary and scattered, like sheep having no shepherd.

1 John 3:16–18
By this we know love, because He laid down His life for us. And we also ought to lay down our lives for the brethren. But whoever has this world's goods, and sees his brother in need, and shuts up his heart from him, how does the love of God abide in him? My little children, let us not love in word or in tongue, but in deed and in truth.

FINISH READING YOUR BOOK AND COMPLETE BOOK REPORT 1 ON THE NEXT PAGE.

DAILY BIBLE READING

✓ Check when completed	
Sunday	Isaiah 44–48
Monday	Isaiah 49–51
Tuesday	Isaiah 52–57
Wednesday	Isaiah 58–62
Thursday	Isaiah 63–66
Friday	Jeremiah 1–6
Saturday	Jeremiah 7–10

BIBLE READING QUESTIONS/THOUGHTS

_____
_____
_____
_____
_____
_____
_____
_____
_____
_____

PRAYER NEEDS THIS WEEK

_____
_____
_____
_____
_____
_____
_____
_____

BOOK REPORT 1

Book title: _____

Author: _____

What did you like about it?

_____
_____
_____
_____

Would you recommend it to others?

_____
_____

What impressed you most about this book?

_____
_____
_____
_____
_____

How did God use the book to speak to you?

_____
_____
_____
_____
_____

Other comments or thoughts about the book:

_____
_____
_____
_____
_____

Lesson *five*

LOVING THE BROKEN

Early in the morning, before my alarm went off, I was suddenly wide awake with a Scripture verse pounding in my mind. "They have no comforter . . . they have no comforter . . . on the side of their oppressors there is power, but they have no comforter . . ."

It was early March 2003, and I had no idea what God was trying to tell me. I looked up the verse and found the whole passage in Ecclesiastes:

> Then I returned and considered all the oppression that is done under the sun:
> And look! The tears of the oppressed,
> But they have no comforter—
> On the side of their oppressors there is power,
> But they have no comforter.
> (Ecclesiastes 4:1)

Still wondering how to apply the Scripture to anything in my life and ministry, I understood the truth of the passage. Oppression and suffering take place all over the world, and God sees more tears than we could imagine. The Bible is full of descriptions of the misery that people have brought on themselves and inflicted on others. God is particularly interested in the sorrows of the weak who suffer at the hands of the strong. In many places, God's Word calls our attention to their needs.

Psalm 146:9

_____

_____

Jeremiah 22:3

_____

_____

God's commission to the church includes expressing all the aspects of who He is and what He has done for us. It's calling rebels to repentance, proclaiming the truth, and showing Jesus as the healer of the broken.

In this chapter we will look at our response to the people around us whose lives are broken. Some of them are victims of injustice and are not responsible for their life circumstances. Others have created their own problems through sin and unwise choices. But God cares for them all and calls us to do the same.

ON THE EQUATOR

Three months after my strange experience during the early morning, a surprise open door in Ecuador brought our team of thirty-two to the Andes Mountains and the capital city of Quito. Our hosts told us that much of our ministry would be reaching out to the children in the poorest neighborhoods there. They explained that the parents of most of the children were drug addicts, alcoholics, thieves, and prostitutes, and they were very concerned about our team's safety in these parts of the city.

We were soon to discover that these children were the ones the Lord had been speaking to me about through Ecclesiastes that morning. Let's correct that—they were *some* of the children. Oppressed children are found in every country, including the United States and Canada. They fill the streets in major cities throughout the world, living out of trash cans and from petty crime. They learn survival skills quickly, or they don't survive long, and when they are dead, few miss them. Life is cheap in much of the world, and parents who abandon their children to the streets are unlikely to mourn their passing. In some major cities in South America, business owners have been known to hire off-duty police to come at night and shoot street children. The businessmen don't want kids around who will steal from them, rob customers, or beg. It's bad for business.

1 Timothy 6:10

_____

_____

Psalm 69:20

_____

_____

Before I tell you more about our team's experience, it's important to say that I don't think Ecuador is worse than any other country. Most people there are kind and friendly. The fact that prostitution is legal and socially acceptable makes it easier for the abuses we discovered to exist, but they are a hidden cancer in the cultures of every other country as well. The team had just never seen the underside of a culture exposed so plainly before.

"THE NEXT TIME I CRY . . ."

It was the first day of the outreach, and we thought we were prepared. We had a well-rehearsed, top-quality program of music and drama in Spanish. Our translators were ready, and everyone else had practiced a limited Spanish vocabulary. Our matching costumes looked sharp, and the PA system was tested. What we hadn't prepared for was the emotional trauma of the children's lives.

The crowded church and attentive children were like the many thousands of others in the many nations where we have presented the gospel. At the end, when we broke into groups with a Spanish translator in each one, things changed. Children began to tell our team stories of the abuse they faced at home. All the stories our hosts had told us about the families and life situations of these children were confirmed.

The little girl in the accompanying photo said to our team, "My mother is a prostitute, but when she brings the men to our house, they are more interested in me than her." It was a story we heard far too many times. She wailed, and our youth held her and cried with her. As horrible as the physical trauma of sexual abuse was, the deeper damage was to her soul and her heart.

The team prayed and sang for her and comforted her, and the Lord directed them with many words of hope and life.

Then she said something we will never forget: *"The next time I cry, I will cry on Jesus."*

This brief sentence speaks volumes. This child knew she would cry again, and with the circumstances in her home, we knew this was true. But for a child about six years old to realize that she could climb onto Jesus' lap just as she had with our kids and cry on Him as she had done with our team was a profound revelation. Truly she would cry again, but she knew where to go with her tears.

Psalm 94:19

_____

_____

Is It Enough?

We ministered to groups of children like this two to four times each day. Leaving the children was so hard each time. Our team knew that they would never see these kids again, and we understood the horrors that many of them would face through the rest of their childhood. Some of our team members were very angry. "We have to do something!" they said. "We have to get them out of there." But the grim reality was that there was nothing we could do to change their circumstances. We had no legal right to take away the children, put them in an orphanage, or bring them to our country.

Our kids asked themselves, and then asked us, whether we had really done any good for the children. Talking, hugging, and praying seemed so intangible in light of the ongoing problems in their lives. We hadn't left them any physical reminders of our presence, and we could take no steps to assure that the abuses they suffered would stop. We knew that we had given them love and a message of hope, but these things seemed so vague and insubstantial in comparison to the reality of their pain.

Our team needed assurance that we were making a genuine difference. In some cases, Christians who see the desperate needs of the broken can take action to correct injustices and shield its victims from further abuse. This includes building orphanages, beginning ministries for street children, sheltering abused women, serving in refugee camps, bringing medical care and education, and using legal and political means to protect the weak. Since our team was made up of teenagers who were in the country for only five weeks, those options were not available to us. Long-term help and changes in the society were needed, but what about that little girl and others like her?

2 Timothy 1:12

_____

_____

1 Peter 1:3–9

_____

_____

It comes down to a question of faith. Do we believe God's love for people is as big as we say it is? Who cares about them more—us or the Lord? A deep awareness of God's compassion and love reassures us that He is more concerned than we are and that we can safely entrust people into His hand after we have done what He sent us to do. The Lord is bigger than our ability to follow up. Part of our responsibility is to hand people over to the next ones who will care for them if at all possible. But sometimes we do our part, thoroughly, and trust Him with the rest.

This is an important point, because the Christian life is full of "chance" encounters with others in which we represent the Lord to them and then are forced to move on. These divine appointments can occur when we're in line at a store or restaurant, seated next to a stranger on a plane, or otherwise crossing paths with someone we don't have an ongoing relationship with. I've had all of the above and many other kinds of situations where the eternal suddenly intrudes into everyday life, and I'm always looking for the next one. It's so exciting to live this way! But they work only if we are confident in the Lord who has sent us and the power of the message we're bringing.

Bearer of hope and truth to serve people trapped in drug addiction and alcoholism. Must seek God for patience and compassion.

Drug addiction and alcoholism are major world issues, contributing to 5.4 percent of the total healthcare burden worldwide. Substance abuse is extremely difficult for people to combat because it can become an uncontrollable mental or physical obsession. Once people become addicted to substances, their bodies can actually require them in order to continue functioning.

Statistics reveal the following:

- Worldwide 2.5 million people die annually from alcohol-related issues.

- 9 percent of all deaths of people between fifteen and twenty-nine can be attributed to alcohol.

- Up to 6.6 percent of people between fifteen and sixty-four are illicit drug users.

- 8.5 percent of adults in the United States are considered to have an alcohol use disorder.

- One out of every one hundred deaths worldwide is due to drug use.

Drug addiction and alcoholism are vital topics for the church to consider, not only because of their direct destruction of millions of lives but also because of their indirect link to many of the other heartbreaking issues around the world. For example, substance abuse is a driving force in the spread of HIV/AIDS, hepatitis B and C, and other fatal diseases. It empowers crime lords who reign over slums and villages, and it perpetuates homelessness. Furthermore, substance abuse plays a major role in the horrors of injustice toward women and children. It is woven through human trafficking, is a prominent factor in domestic abuse, and is linked to child abandonment.

Addictions begin when someone uses an artificial substance as a means to pacify a deeper emotional, physical, or spiritual longing. As Christians, we must view substance abuse with the lens that we use for all other destructive habits: we are sinners, in need of the saving power of Jesus. We must choose to look at addicts with deep compassion and love, knowing that Jesus is the only One capable of truly satisfying our longings, filling our voids, and making us whole. People who are trapped in addiction must be pointed to the Savior for healing and rehabilitation.

It's your world—do something today!

Teen Challenge, a Christ-centered drug and alcohol rehabilitation center, has over 199 centers in the United States and is present in eighty-three countries around the world. There are many ways to volunteer, including leading Bible studies, cooking, and fundraising for the center. Go to *www.teenchallenge.net* to find a center near you.

John 10:27–29

_____

_____

Hebrews 4:12

_____

_____

We Have a Comforter

The people we encounter may not have a comforter, but we do. Jesus promised the Holy Spirit to the church. He came on the day of Pentecost and hasn't left since.

John 14:16

_____

_____

John 14:26

_____

_____

But why did Jesus send us the Holy Spirit, the Comforter? To make us more comfortable? To add to our personal peace and affluence? No! The Comforter's role is to be the presence of God with us at all times, to teach us and point us to Jesus. Everything He does in us, He wants to do for everyone else. God does not play favorites.

Think of it! Has the Lord restored you from when your life was in ruins? Has He healed your broken heart? Helped you forgive those who have hurt you? Washed away your bitterness and hatred? Has He restored your sense of value and given you a purpose for living? Has He removed your fears and anxiety and helped you face life with the confidence that comes from knowing He is with you?

They have no comforter. We have a Comforter. Are we keeping Him to ourselves?

You Have Known My Soul in Adversities

We have all needed the comfort God gives. Being a Christian doesn't mean things always go smoothly. Jesus gave us many promises, and one is that in the world we would have tribulation (John 16:33). There are many reasons why we go through hard times. Sometimes we bring them on ourselves by bad decisions, and we reap what we have sown. At other times we suffer because of the bad choices of people around us. Sometimes we don't know what is going on, and our faith is stretched to the limit. We may never in this lifetime understand the whys of our lives, but God is working in all these things to create depth and strength in our relationship with Him.

Psalm 31:7

_____

_____

He draws near in our hardest times, even when we can't feel His presence. It may seem like God disappears in our darkest moments, but He is the reason we survive those times and the reason we don't fall away.

Lamentations 3:22

_____

_____

Looking back, we can see that we have a Comforter. Now God calls us to pass along the comfort we have received to the needy people we meet. We can tell them that even if we haven't experienced the depths of the sufferings they are going through, we serve a faithful God who keeps His word. We can tell them the stories of how He has intervened in our lives. We can tell them that they can cry on Jesus.

Isaiah 40:1–2

_____

_____

2 Corinthians 1:3–5

_____

_____

Stuck in the Tar

About twenty years ago a contractor friend of mine and two hired men put new shingles on my roof. I spent a long day of hard work up there with them, and the next day I climbed up the ladder to look at my new roof. Out of the corner of my eye, I saw something moving. It was a sparrow, stuck in the fresh tar near the air conditioner. When I walked closer, he panicked. The poor bird was already in a terrible situation and must have thought I was there to finish him off.

Climbing down the ladder, I ran to the kitchen and got some warm, soapy water in a basin. I went back up and pulled the terrified bird free, but the tar was all over him. I spoke to him gently, but I don't speak sparrow and couldn't communicate that I was only trying to help. I felt so much compassion for this little creature, but he didn't understand. He was trying desperately to get away from the only help he had as I carefully washed the tar from his feathers. At last, with a great shuddering gasp, the bird stopped breathing.

I know you were hoping to hear that the tar came off his feathers and the bird soared away to join his family. Did this story's ending make you sad? Some hard-hearted types may say it was only a bird, but if this true story had been about a puppy, they would probably be in tears. God used this event to show me how much compassion He has on us.

Psalm 102:1, 7

_____

_____

Matthew 10:29, 31

_____

_____

Although sparrows are insignificant to people, they are valuable to God. Is it too far-fetched to wonder if God directed my steps to find this desperate little bird, not just to teach me a lesson but because He even cared for a dying sparrow? God cares about people so much more.

Luke 12:6–7

_____

_____

When a sparrow gets caught in the tar, it takes more than another sparrow to get him out. In the same way, people caught in the bondage of their sins need more than another person to get them out. Human sympathy won't do it. A handout isn't enough. Philosophies and psychology can't clear away the wreckage of a human life and put it back on track. Only Jesus can solve this problem.

Compassion versus Judgment

I had just finished making some copies at OfficeMax when a voice said, "Excuse me." I turned to see a young woman walking in my direction. She had obviously been beaten up. Makeup didn't quite hide the black eye or the swollen and bruised cheeks. The moment I saw her, I felt an incredible surge of God's compassion. She said rapidly, "My car ran out of gas, and I need just two dollars. Can you help me?" My heart told me she was not telling the truth, but the compassion was so powerful I reached for my wallet very slowly. She pointed to a car and told me it was hers—probably a lie. I continued to get my wallet out very slowly. I asked her name. By now my wallet was in plain sight.

There are two ways of looking at this situation. I could have told myself that this young woman would probably spend the money on heroin or meth and told her no. On the other hand, for only two dollars I could witness to the woman at the well.

Still moving very slowly to stall for time, I asked her where she worked.

"I'm a topless dancer at the XXX Club," she said. "Have you ever been there?"

Now I was caught off guard and surprised, so I pulled out the two dollars and stammered, "No, I'm a Christian . . ." and in a split second she turned to run. The fear on her face told me what "Christian" meant for her: people who judge me, people who think I'm bad, people who call me a whore.

But before she ran off, she saw the two dollars and froze. God was present there, and I kept talking very gently. "God has something better for you. You are very precious to Him." A look of surprise came over her face as I gave her the money. As she walked away, she paused to turn and thank me. "Not for the money," she added, "but for what you said."

I've prayed for this woman and for others like her nearly every day since then, but I've never gone to visit her at work! That day, God wanted to show a lost girl His heart for her. Sure, God wants her to change her sinful lifestyle, but she already knew she was a sinner. What she didn't know was that God and His people care for her.

Alcoholics and drug addicts; little girls selling their bodies and souls; street children who live by their wits, stealing and begging to survive; wretched street people; shivering homeless; mothers trying to rock their hungry children to sleep; glue sniffers; the mentally ill; the demonized; women and children beaten by abusive, drunken men; human trafficking victims; refugees; oppressed minority groups; the estimated twenty-seven million slaves in the world today; faces with expressions of hopelessness, fear, emptiness, rejection, and pain; faces that show loss of family, job, security, home, dignity; those who have seen too much pain and trouble and injustice—how the Father's heart breaks as He sees the destruction in the lives of His creations! God wants to put His arms around all of these people— through us. But He can't if we judge them. They are sparrows caught in the tar, but Jesus can set them free and restore them.

All over the world, right now, God sees it all. All day long, every single day.

Proverbs 15:3

_____

_____

Exodus 3:7

_____

_____

Isaiah 63:9

_____

_____

Will you ask the Father for eyes to see people the way He sees them? Do you know any sparrows caught in the tar of their sins? They are infinitely valuable to the Father, regardless of how degraded their lifestyles are. The most hopeless derelict can have a better future in Jesus. No one is beyond His reach.

Is there anyone in your life whose lifestyle of sin is repulsive to you? A family member who has worn you out, someone you once tried to help but have now written off? A person you despise who seems beyond hope?

When you see the cardboard-sign carriers or a drunk passed out somewhere, what springs up in your heart? The love of God or a feeling of revulsion? What's your response? Do you turn away from need like the priest and Pharisee on the road to Jericho or toward the need like the Good Samaritan? The Lord hasn't written those people off, no matter how revolting or awful their sin may be. There's a place for them in God's presence.

Psalm 84:3

_____

_____

When we first come to Christ, God begins to transform our lives. The most obvious areas of sin go first: immorality, drugs and alcohol, crime, and so on. But we tend to keep a few of the more "acceptable" kinds of sin: pride, judging others, gossip, and self-righteousness. If the topless dancer story brings up a haughty protest in your heart, it's time to face these things.

You may say that there's a great difference between the six-year-old forced into prostitution and the woman who works at the topless bar, and you're right. The girl has no responsibility before the Lord for sin at her age and in her circumstances, while the adult clearly does. Yet God's heart breaks for both of them.

Think for a minute, not about what the prostitute does, but about why she does it and how she got there. Obviously this isn't a career option a young woman sets out to pursue. In ordinary circumstances, it wouldn't be a choice for any girl. So what brought her into this situation? Like a sparrow caught in the tar, I'm sure she wasn't expecting to be caught in circumstances this destructive and deadly, and she likely didn't know how to get out of them. Was she sexually abused by a drunken father growing up? Or used by many? Is she under the emotional domination of evil men? Did drug addiction and desperation drive her to this? Certainly that would have entailed a sinful choice.

Here is where injustice and responsibility collide in the life of broken people. Let's let God sort it out, and let's be sure to tell them and others like them that there is a Savior who calls them to come.

Wrap-up

Let's put the illustration of the sparrow and the tar into a fresh prayer that sums up all we have seen so far.

God, let the things that break Your heart break my heart too! Don't let me be callous and shallow. Don't let me think of my own comforts when a desperate world cries out. Don't let me live for myself. Help me to see the people caught in the bondage of their sins. Show me the hurting ones whom I might overlook. Make my heart sensitive to Your voice and tender enough to break when Your heart breaks. I know I pass by people in need of You every day. Don't let my ears be deaf to their cries. In Jesus' name. Amen.

What stands out to you in this prayer?

_____

_____

How will you put it into practice?

_____

_____

What has God been saying to you this week?

_____

_____

How does this affect your daily life?

_____

_____

How does this affect your life plans?

_____

_____

SCRIPTURE MEMORY

Proverbs 28:1
The wicked flee when no one
    pursues,
But the righteous are bold as
    a lion.

1 John 4:4
You are of God, little children,
and have overcome them,
because He who is in you is
greater than he who is in the
world.

DAILY BIBLE READING

✓ Check when completed	
Sunday	Jeremiah 11–15
Monday	Jeremiah 16–20
Tuesday	Jeremiah 21–25
Wednesday	Jeremiah 26–29
Thursday	Jeremiah 30–33
Friday	Jeremiah 34–35
Saturday	Jeremiah 36–37

BIBLE READING QUESTIONS/THOUGHTS

_____
_____
_____
_____
_____
_____
_____
_____
_____
_____
_____

PRAYER NEEDS THIS WEEK

_____
_____
_____
_____
_____
_____
_____
_____
_____

6

Lesson six
How to Be a Mighty Man or Woman of God

Have you ever been inspired by the stories of great men and women of God and wondered what made them what they were? All through history we see people who are set before us as examples—people who lived life fully and bore fruit and who were really like Jesus, not just all talk and no action. If you have never been inspired by one of God's heroes, watch the movie *End of the Spear* or read *Bruchko, Vanya, Peace Child,* or *Lords of the Earth.*

Now, have you also wondered whether there is any hope for ordinary people like you and me to be the source of inspiration for future generations? How do you get there?

The body of Christ needs heroes today, people of courage and sacrifice, whose lives can be models for the rest to follow. Even if we don't make the history books or the news, how can our lives count for the King and the kingdom?

The goal of being a hero of the kingdom is not fame or power. Heaven is not about status and reputation, and serving God while living on earth is not about riches or egos. There's no problem with being a hero in the body of Christ as long as we don't think of ourselves as heroes. We just want to hear, "Well done, good and faithful servant. . . . Enter into the joy of your [L]ord" (Matthew 25:23). It's all about serving, loving, and obeying, and when the rewards are distributed in heaven, we will cast our crowns before Him (Revelation 4:10). Don't you want to find out now what it will be like then? Are you interested in being prepared so that when you stand before Him, you can be confident, not ashamed (1 John 2:28)? There's no rewind in heaven. Once we breathe our final breath, it will be too late to change anything.

Who Are the Mighty?

Let's look back three thousand years to a time of war. There was no Facebook, no TV news, no Twitter to find out about people, so stories about the battles were passed on by word of mouth. Let me give you a picture of this era.

Out of the thousands of soldiers in King David's army, three great men were the heroes of the people. All the little boys pretended to be one of the three mighty men, using sticks as swords and arguing about who would play the heroes. "I had to be a Philistine yesterday, so you have to be the bad guy today. I get to be one of the three mighty men." As the girls got water from the village wells, people in the market would be discussing the latest news from the front lines. The girls would whisper to each other, "I saw one of the three warriors once. He was so handsome. I hope I marry someone as amazing as him."

What made these men such great heroes?

Scripture says, "These are the names of the mighty men whom David had: Josheb-Basshebeth the Tachmonite, chief among the captains. He was called Adino the Eznite, because he had killed eight hundred men at one time" (2 Samuel 23:8). Adino must have been huge. Picture the rippling muscles of a comic book superhero. Swinging a sword all day and chopping people's heads off is hard work! Notice that Scripture doesn't say that God helped Adino in the battle (though we'll see that the other two warriors did receive divine assistance). His ability was something Adino had naturally that made him a great hero.

But if being mighty for God required physical size and strength, if it required natural abilities beyond everyone else's, virtually all of us would be disqualified. Most of God's people are just ordinary people. They're just regular folk. In fact, some who are spectacular in their abilities may never humble their hearts before God. If they have it all together, from their prideful perspective, why would they need the Lord?

1 Corinthians 1:26

_____

_____

Does God call the mighty, or does He make the called mighty? You may want to reread that last sentence and think about it. There's a huge difference.

Have you ever heard the discouraging voice of the enemy saying that you'll never do anything for God? That you'll never amount to anything spiritually, never get your act together?

God has always called regular people, from Bible days to modern days. He's not looking for the exceptional, just for people who will respond to His grace and love and humble their hearts before Him. He chooses the foolish things of the world to confound the wise (1 Corinthians 1:27). He looks for those who will simply obey Him, and then He steps in to work through them. Human perfection isn't required.

Let's be honest. How many of us are still struggling with some of the same sins we were fighting five or ten years ago? My hand went up first! It's still all about God's grace in my life, and yours too. I haven't conquered all of my giants yet. If you have, please write to me and tell me your secret.

TAKING A STAND

Size made Adino a hero. Maybe we can't relate to him, but there are two more mighty warriors to whom we can relate. The first of these is Eleazar.

And after him was Eleazar the son of Dodo [Let's just stop right there so you can thank God for your name!], the Ahohite, one of the three mighty men with David when they defied the Philistines who were gathered there for battle, and the men of Israel had retreated. He arose and attacked the Philistines until his hand was weary, and his hand stuck to the sword. The Lord brought about a great victory that day; and the people returned after him only to plunder. (2 Samuel 23:9–10)

What made Eleazar stand out? When the rest of God's people ran backward, he was the only one still there. Sometimes obeying the Lord means going it alone, but the good news is that God doesn't leave us alone for long. If we're going to take a stand for the Lord, it may seem lonely at the moment, but look at the Scripture: "The Lord brought about a great victory that day." God came to the battlefield to stand with Eleazar.

We live in a time of battle too, and often God's people retreat. When the others chickened out,

Eleazar went forward. Choice made him a hero. I've had some memorable chicken-outs in my life. What about you? List one here:

_____

_____

List another:

_____

_____

Do you need more paper?

Eleazar wasn't a hero because of his size; he was a hero because of his stand. When do we take a stand? When do we draw a line in the sand and say, "This far but no farther"? We all face those times

---

True Story

What's the greatest danger you have faced in serving the Lord? Here's what happened to me during my second outreach to Haiti.

After a great week of leadership training, youth camp, and outreach, things got a little too exciting the last day. Returning to the capital city in a packed minivan, we came up to a protest against the government blocking the two-lane dirt road that is their Highway One. An older man standing nearby told us the alternate route through a village was also blocked but that he would come and get us through. Then he left and didn't return, so we continued ahead on the alternate route. We saw a large crowd of mostly young people blocking the village road.

As we drove closer, the protestors surrounded the van and started waving machetes, shouting in anger. One large young man with a bottle in one hand and a machete in the other—obviously their leader—was especially enraged and possibly demonized. He was wearing a blue shirt and black pants. Remember this point. He stood on a barricade of thick tree branches that prevented us from driving through. We were all praying out loud and quoting God's promises for protection, but it looked bad. I knew that if we only got robbed, it would be a good day. I was very concerned for the safety of a Canadian missionary girl from our staff who was in the van. Only a quarter inch of glass separated us from the screaming, machete-waving crowd. The mob looked toward their leader, waiting for orders. Recalling Haiti's customs of bloody revenge and brutality led us to pray some serious prayers.

Psalm 86:14: A mob of violent men have sought my life.

My good friend, a Haitian YWAMer and pastor, was driving. I've stayed in his home and he's stayed in mine. He got out of the car to talk to the leader while others yelled at us through the windows. With real concern, I asked the Lord what we should do if he started whacking my friend. There was no way that I could have rescued him if an attack began. I knew I'd be dead before I ever reached the front of the van. The man clad in blue and black raised his machete over my friend's head, shouting in his language, and my friend came back to the van, saying that the man refused to let us through. The leader shouted more things and the crowd went into a frenzy. I could see that the situation was just about to pop.

Just then the older man roared up on a motorcycle, jumped off, and got right in the young guy's face. The leader didn't like what the old man was saying and waved the machete while shouting things we couldn't understand, and I thought, *This man came to save us, and now he might die for it!* The young man finally backed down. The older man cleared the barricade of rocks and branches, and we went through.

One of my coworkers in El Paso told me that while I was gone, she was praying for me and saw swirling evil in blue and black. When the Lord leads you to pray for missionaries, don't ignore Him.

Psalm 121:2–3, 7–8:
My help comes from the LORD, . . .

He who keeps you will not slumber.
The Lord shall preserve you from all evil; . . .
The Lord shall preserve your going out and
your coming in.

When that road intersected Highway One again, we came upon the main protest. Traffic was backed up, and hundreds of people were standing around. We needed to go around a bus with flattened tires that was blocking the road. On the other side of it was a fast-moving river with no guardrail, and the space looked too narrow for us to pass. Many helpful Haitian people—they are generally very friendly—tried to guide us.

Just then I saw smoke on the far side of the bus. Government troops had arrived and sent tear gas into the crowd. Suddenly people were screaming and crying and running our way. Then the shooting started. Apparently responding to one of the protesters who had fired first, the soldiers opened fire with M16s. The running and screaming intensified. One boy dove into the river, and complete panic engulfed the crowd. There was no time to be scared; we were just asking God which way we should go to avoid getting shot.

The troops threw a man to the ground, surrounded him and kicked him brutally until he stopped moving. They motioned for the vehicles to come through. We squeezed around the bus and passed the tense soldiers in full battle gear with their fingers on the triggers.

Psalm 55:9: I have seen violence and strife in the city.

Psalm 68:20: To God the Lord belong escapes from death.

After that everything was fine. By the time we got to the airport, we had missed our flight, but we caught another and eventually made it home. It was my birthday. The next day I was glad to celebrate at home with my family. God had been faithful to protect us. Through the whole situation, I felt only the seriousness of the crisis that caused me to pray hard, but never fear. At times like this we need to hear from the Lord. Our focus was on trusting the Lord and asking Him what to do next. Experiences like this are the reason we ask so many people to pray for our trips.

and situations when we know we have to say, "*Enough!*" There are incidents in our daily lives when we must take a stand, and either we choose to retreat or we move forward.

God provides courage in times when we need it. He doesn't leave us alone in battle. We don't care about recognition coming from men, but we look for recognition from God. We want God to notice us from heaven and help us. We want to be the ones God comes to stand with on the battlefield. He's looking for people like that.

2 Chronicles 16:9a

Eleazar arose and attacked. There are times when we can't just stay put: situations that demand that God's people be aggressive, stepping out of our comfort zone and into our fears, going to the place where God calls even if it's scary and lonely. We can make excuses why we can't and give God reasons why we shouldn't. Have you ever prayed until an opportunity was safely past and then told the Lord that you were ready?

There are times when we took a stand and times when we didn't. It is the difference between those two extremes that determines whether or not we will have crowns to cast before the Lord (Revelation 3:11). These are choices that will earn us a reward in heaven, or not, and they will make us examples to others, or not. When God replays the video of our lives, will we say, "I never stepped forward. I never went from my comfort zone into the fear zone and into the lonely zone, because I didn't trust that God would meet me on the battlefield"?

This stepping forward is the place where faith grows. God is found right on the edge of our faith. Each of us has what I call our comfortable faith. It's the things that we don't have to stretch very far to believe. "Give us this day our daily bread" is one of these. How many of us, if we were born in a place like America, have really had to trust the Lord for food? Our situation is very different from much of the body of Christ around the world who really do have to believe for their next meal. It's not too hard to believe that God will keep us safe in North America, but prayer for safety is much more real to believers in Sudan or Iran.

When we go past our comfortable faith to the edge of faith, it's time for putting God and His promises to the test. This is the perspiring, heart-pounding level of faith. It's the "If God doesn't come through, then I'm in real trouble" place of faith, and that's where faith really grows and where we see God's intervention.

Picture God in heaven, looking down on the earth. He hears lots of monotonous prayers, sent upward as a formality before meals or bedtime. Contrast these with the sight of Eleazar, or you or me, standing alone before impossible odds—or maybe just facing the social pressure of people snickering or rolling their eyes at our "naive" faith. If we call out for divine help in situations like these, don't you think that kind of prayer will gain God's attention?

Proverbs 28:1

_____

_____

We make a lot of excuses for ourselves when we hear messages like this. "I'm just a shy person," we rationalize, "and some people are more cut out for this kind of thing. I would just get my words all mixed up and get confused if I tried to stand up for God publicly. Other people are cut out for that missionary stuff and witnessing and all that. I think I'll just stay home and pray." Jesus did the work to make us righteous children of God, to make us what we weren't before. Can you trust Him to fulfill the rest of this promise and make you as bold as a lion?

After the battle was over, the people came to plunder the bodies of the fallen Philistines. The Hebrew word there means "to strip off." Dead soldiers don't put up much of a fight. Imagine the soldiers going home that night, carrying the weapons and jewels they took from corpses. They plopped down the gold, the clothes, the best the Philistine malls had to offer, on the kitchen table. Their little boys said, "Daddy, did you kill a lot of Philistines today? Tell me about the battle!"

The men had stripped all this from the soldiers' bodies, but they weren't responsible for those bodies—Eleazar was. Maybe they lied and claimed great bravery in the face of certain death, but in their heart of hearts they knew they were cowards. They may have said, "You should have seen me out there today, son!" while thinking, _I'm glad he couldn't see me out there today._ Or maybe they were honest and said, "Son, I have to admit: I had a great view of the battle from up in a tree. It was all Eleazar and God. Eleazar couldn't carry all the gold home, so I got some."

There will always be plenty of people to claim a share of the reward, but where are the ones who lead the charge? Do you just want a share of the reward or a share of the battle? It's very different returning to plunder after someone else has won a battle, versus having God come to our sides in the midst of the battle and bring us victory.

TRUSTING IN GOD'S FAITHFULNESS

Now we turn to the third mighty man of God: Shammah.

> And after him was Shammah the son of Agee the Hararite. The Philistines had gathered together into a troop where there was a piece of ground full of lentils. So the people fled from the Philistines. But [Shammah] stationed himself in the middle of the field, defended it, and killed the Philistines. And the LORD brought about a great victory. (2 Samuel 23:11–12)

Doesn't this sound like a rerun of the last story? Why did God's soldiers run the second time? Maybe they weren't the same ones as in the last battle, but if they had seen that God comes through for those who stand for Him, it should have given them courage to stay with Shammah. Maybe Shammah had seen Eleazar's stand and drew courage from it. We don't know for sure, but we can apply this in our own lives. Will we learn from our failures, from our running away, to stand next time? Will we take courage from the people we have seen stand for the Lord and follow their example?

Shammah wouldn't back down. Choice made him a hero. This is taking the risk to do something we don't know if we can do. It's taking the risk to do something we've never done before. It's thinking that God may or may not fulfill His promise, and not knowing for sure until we're on the battlefield alone with God and our enemies. It's do or die, when God has to come through or we're dead meat—that's when we find out that He's as faithful as He promised to be.

Have you seen evidence in your own life that the Lord is faithful? List a few times that He has come through for you.

_____

_____

Revelation 19:11

_____

_____

I'm sure the temptation came to Shammah to run with the rest of the Israelites. "It's only a bean field, not the king's palace . . . is it worth taking a stand? . . . why risk your life for beans? . . . let someone else do it . . . nobody else cares."

The whispers in Shammah's mind to save himself—just like the people's taunts when Jesus was on the cross—are the same temptations we encounter today: let someone else make the sacrifice, spare yourself the trouble, take the easy way out, melt into the crowd, you won't stand out if everybody's running, just join them. Shammah's well-meaning friends probably looked over their shoulders as they retreated and yelled, "Shammah, are you crazy? RUN!" But Shammah didn't listen, and God came to join him on that bean field.

Seeing a lone Israelite on the battlefield, the Philistines charged forward. With bloodlust in their eyes, they prepared to take out all of their hatred of Israel on one lone soldier. The enemy is always emboldened when God's people run. But imagine their bravado turning to terror as they see that this is no ordinary soldier. He was just not going down. As the Philistine corpses began to pile up around Shammah, the soldiers' premature shouts of victory turned into cries for mercy.

How did God do it? I don't know. Maybe He made Shammah arrow-proof. I can picture the arrows just bouncing off him. It was like something out of Smallville. Can you picture Shammah thundering, "Bwahahaha! Shoot me again!"

Shammah's friends were already mourning the loss of their fellow soldier. With tears in their eyes, but safely hidden in trees and behind buildings, they turned to watch his last moments. Imagine their shock when they saw something supernatural happening. Amidst the trampled lentil plants, Shammah used his sword or bow with devastating effect and skill they had never seen before. God was with him! The shouts of victory were in Hebrew, not Philistine.

DEFENDING OUR BATTLEFIELD

This story is about more than beans. Every bit of ground relinquished to the enemy is added to his domain. Whatever we concede, whatever we give up when we back up, becomes part of the growing domain of darkness. It's harder to get it back than to keep it in the first place.

1 John 5:19

_____

_____

Ephesians 4:27

_____

_____

We're giving up a bean field here and a bean field there. We have given place to the devil in our emotions, our minds, our lives, and our families. Once we allow the devil to occupy, it's hard to kick him out! It's easier to keep him out in the first place, because God stands with us when we defend the turf that is ours. Defend and stand your ground. Don't give it up without a fight.

All of us have been assigned a battlefield. I can't defend your bean field, and I am not called to do so. Each of us has our own responsibility. Yours may be large or small, look important or unimportant, but it's your job to keep that ground for God. Maybe it's being salt and light in your office, store, restaurant, or classroom. It definitely includes your home and family. What would the world and the church be like if we kept the ground assigned to us and didn't lose any to the devil, and went forward to gain more ground for the kingdom? What if we each followed the example of the mighty warriors?

Do you want God to join you on your battlefield? Then take a stand. Remember this: _Christians don't back up._ We stand for righteousness.

Taking just one battlefield as an example, what if we all spoke up when the talk around us got unholy, blasphemous, or ungodly? We think the nice, Christian thing to do is just wait quietly until they change the subject. Enough of niceness! Being nice is not a fruit of the Spirit. We are niced to death. In the face of evil, if we're nice and sweet, does that show the Lord's nature? I don't think so, because the Lord is a warrior. He is mighty in battle (Exodus 15:3; Psalm 24:8; 144:1). We should show all the fruit

Refugee camp volunteer to serve victims of war. Preferably someone who will endure difficult living conditions because they are driven by mercy and love.

Refugees—people who seek protection because they are persecuted based on race, national origin, beliefs, or political opinion—face some of the most difficult trials of any population. After fleeing violence or being forcibly removed from their country, these displaced people are usually put into refugee camps, which are makeshift cities, often in another nation. Inside these camps, refugees face extremely vulnerable circumstances—they are separated from family and entirely dependent on humanitarian aid. Refugees are usually not allowed outside the camps, and many times, the host country itself is struggling with poverty, famine, and drought. Without opportunity to grow crops or search for water, people in a refugee camp are at the mercy of the host country, begging for whatever resources that country is able to give. Refugees' talents, capabilities, and livelihoods are stripped from them, and they rarely have the opportunity to work. Because the majority of refugees are women or children, they are especially vulnerable to attacks such as rape or abuse. Compounding all of this is the rampant spread of disease

from sewage disposal problems and close living conditions.

In 1994, one million people from Rwanda escaped genocide and moved to a refugee camp in Zaire (now the Republic of the Congo). However, shortly afterward, sixty thousand of these people died from water shortages and disease within the refugee camp. The United Nations has since set up regulations for refugee camps, and one rule is that there must be one water tap for every one hundred people and one toilet for every twenty people. Take a moment to thank God for the multiple sinks and toilets you have in your home! Let the reality of the plight of refugees sink in:

- The United Nations counted 43.3 million people who were forcibly displaced from their homes in 2010.
- Of this number, 27.1 million remained in their native countries but were unable to live in their homes because of natural disasters or civil unrest.
- Another 15.2 million people were refugees, and 983,000 were asylum seekers (people waiting to be approved for refugee status).
- Around 12 million people have no country in which they claim citizenship.
- Women and children make up roughly 80 percent of all refugees.

JoRae Dabbs always had a heart for the downtrodden and outcast, and after high school and some missions trips with King's Kids El Paso, she decided to study human rights law. Her first summer in law school, JoRae got an internship helping children who come to the United States by themselves. It was there that she met Abdi (not his real name), a twenty-four-year-old seeking to become a refugee in the

United States. Abdi was originally from Ethiopia but had a Somali background. When he was sixteen years old, extreme tension grew between Somalia and Ethiopia, and Abdi's family was heavily persecuted. His father was imprisoned and murdered, and as the oldest of his siblings, Abdi was arrested. After being tortured by the police, Abdi fled Ethiopia. For the next eight years, his journey took him through Kenya, South Africa, Brazil, and Mexico. Abdi eventually ended up on the Texas border, where he met JoRae.

JoRae recognized that if she didn't fight for Abdi, no one else would. He had no hope, because at every point in his life, someone had taken advantage of him. JoRae made the commitment to show him the love of Jesus in the practical setting of the courtroom and therefore turn the tide of his life. JoRae won his case! Abdi still keeps in touch with JoRae and her family.

It's your world—do something today!

Volunteer with World Relief, a Christian organization that connects churches to refugees in the United States. Go to *www.worldrelief.org* for more information. Additionally, you can search the Internet to see if there are any facilities that aid refugees near you. Even though the standards are significantly better in the United States, living here is bittersweet for refugees. It is a new culture and language, and they have suffered tremendous loss. They need the love and hope of Jesus to walk them through this tragic time.

There are multiple YWAM programs aimed at refugees, such as the Rescue Ops school and the Justice & Compassion school, and the opportunity to tutor and serve refugees. Go to *www.ywam.org* for more information.

of the Spirit (Galatians 5:22–23), but that doesn't mean that we shouldn't stand. Remember the armor of God in Ephesians 6:10–17? We are to use the shield of faith, the sword of the Spirit, the helmet of salvation. Does your Bible list the polo shirt of niceness? No!

I'm not encouraging you to be obnoxious, combative, or difficult, and certainly not judgmental in a "holier than thou," prideful way. I'm encouraging you to stand for God so that people will draw courage from your example. When we stand our ground, plenty of God's soldiers will come back to join in the plunder. Those who ran before will return when they see the victory.

1 Samuel 14:22

_____

_____

Living by Faith or Fear

This is not just a history lesson. These stories are designed to give us courage. If God was a mighty warrior then, what is He now?

Malachi 3:6

_____

_____

Hebrews 13:8

_____

_____

All the other soldiers in King David's army had the same opportunities to become heroes of the people. Three thousand years later we remember the three. Their names and stories are printed in the Bible to inspire all generations. Think of it—God's Word is eternal. It's settled forever in heaven, and it contains the names of ordinary people who took a stand, because God wanted to honor them and inspire us. The three saw their chance and went for it. Will we do the same?

There were thousands of other soldiers in the army at that time. What were their names? Who knows? They ran, and that was the end of the story for them. We are also faced with decisions. Will we go backward or forward? Will we live by faith or fear? Will we follow the crowd or lead the crowd? Ultimately it's a question of faith. Do we value the eternal more than the temporary? Is God's opinion of us more important than man's? Would we rather please the Lord or please people?

Sometimes while Christians sleep, sometimes while Christians play, sometimes while Christians run, the enemy advances to take whatever he can from us. The devil's goal is still to steal, kill, and destroy.

John 10:10

_____

_____

Our enemy is the devil and darkness in whatever form it manifests itself. The enemy gets bolder when he sees God's people run. But God's people get bolder when they see someone take a stand.

Often we don't run in retreat. Satan isn't taking over ground in huge leaps—it's just a little slide, then another little slide. But keep sliding, and eventually he gets it all. The results are the same as if we had just run away in the first place. If God called His people to take a stand then, what does He call us to do now? Ooze? Go with the flow? I don't think so. But because we've done that for so long, the world is the way it is now. We've forgotten that.

1 John 4:4

_____

_____

In our lives, in our families, in our society, it's stand or slide. In our personal lives, are we slowly moving backwards? We slide back, slide back . . . backslide. Take this one-question test: Do you allow things in your life now that would have horrified you a few years ago?

2 Corinthians 13:5

_____

_____

Maybe you won't have the opportunity to change all of your society, turn the course of the media, or affect global situations, but you still have your bean field. No excuses for making excuses! God supplies the courage for taking a stand whenever we need it. He gives the boldness for going forward and not retreating. We don't have to be bullied into surrender, compliance, or silence.

Some of you feel a stirring inside. Something is pumping. You know you're called to *do* something. What will happen on your bean field?

Wrap-up

Let's wrap this up and apply it to our own lives. Let's put the teachings into a fresh prayer that sums up all we have seen in this chapter.

Father, I've backed up way too much. I've let intimidation, the opinions of others, and every other device of Satan convince me to hang back, keep quiet, give up, and run away. But, Lord, I'm tired of this, and I don't want to make any more excuses. Today, I call upon You to make me bold, with strength in my soul. Help me, Lord! In Jesus' name. Amen.

What stands out to you in this prayer?

_____

_____

How will you put it into practice?

_____

_____

What has God been saying to you this week?

_____

_____

How does this affect your daily life?

_____

_____

How does this affect your life plans?

_____

_____

SCRIPTURE MEMORY

Luke 6:46
But why do you call Me "Lord, Lord," and do not do the things which I say?

Isaiah 66:1–2
"Heaven is My throne,
And earth is My footstool.
Where is the house that you
   will build Me?
And where is the place of My
   rest?
For all those things My hand
   has made,
And all those things exist,"
Says the LORD.
"But on this one will I look:
On him who is poor and of a
   contrite spirit,
And who trembles at My
   word."

DAILY BIBLE READING

✓ Check when completed	
Sunday	Jeremiah 38–39
Monday	Jeremiah 40–45
Tuesday	Jeremiah 46–52
Wednesday	Lamentations 1–5
Thursday	Ezekiel 1–6
Friday	Ezekiel 7–11
Saturday	Ezekiel 12–15

BIBLE READING QUESTIONS/THOUGHTS

_____
_____
_____
_____
_____
_____
_____
_____
_____
_____
_____

PRAYER NEEDS THIS WEEK

_____
_____
_____
_____
_____
_____
_____
_____

7

THE KING'S DESIRE

My father was a high-ranking army officer. He had a sign in his office that said, "Eternal vigilance is the price of freedom." This means that in order to stay free, nations can't let down their guard and kick back. Sworn enemies don't just give up. Just as the Philistines hated Israel three thousand years ago, Israel's current enemies are dedicated to the nation's destruction. America's enemies are also lurking and plotting, so our government employs thousands of people to keep our country safe.

You and I have *spiritual* enemies who have a single-minded purpose: our harm. Their goal is to discourage our walk with God, hinder our work for the Lord, afflict us with every possible kind of suffering, rob us of joy, obscure our faith, tax our patience, destroy our vision, and generally make life miserable.

1 Peter 5:8

_____

_____

Have you let your guard down? Your adversary the devil is looking to see what he can take over. He doesn't play fair. There are no gentlemen's rules in this battle, unlike in movies about the chivalrous days of great sea battles and "civil" wars. This is an enemy who fights dirty, kicks you when you're down, and uses every tactic at his disposal, plus thousands of years of experience, to try to defeat you.

The good news is this: God is on your side. He makes mighty warriors from ordinary, flawed, struggling, imperfect men and women like you and me.

FACING THE ENEMY

Let's pick up the story from 2 Samuel that we looked at in the previous lesson:

> Then three of the thirty chief men went down at harvest time and came to David at the cave of Adullam. And the troop of Philistines encamped in the Valley of Rephaim. David was then in the stronghold, and the garrison of the Philistines was then in Bethlehem. And David said with longing, "Oh, that someone would give me a drink of the water from the well of Bethlehem, which is by the gate!" (2 Samuel 23:13–15)

The garrison of the Philistines was in Bethlehem, and the three mighty men had gone to King David. David's stronghold was a cave, but a cave is not a fitting place for the king of the nation to hide. David didn't want to be in hiding anyway. He was used to battle.

Bethlehem was the city of his family and the place where God had first proclaimed that David would be king (1 Samuel 16). And as Micah would prophesy a couple of centuries later, it would someday be the place where the Messiah would be born (Micah 5:2). But now it was under enemy control. Bethlehem was small but significant. Calling it a city is generous; by our standards it was just a village.

Since it was David's home, however, its value was huge as a symbol both to the Jews and to the conquering Philistines who lived there. Think in modern terms: How would America feel if an enemy army had taken over and moved into any city in our country? It would become the primary goal to retrieve it from their control.

Bethlehem wasn't even near the border of the Philistines. They had ventured far into Israel to take it over, and it was a prize to them. David wanted Bethlehem back.

Have you lost ground to the enemy? Is there some area of your life in which you used to have victory but now you're defeated? Does he occupy territory that should rightfully belong to the Lord?

Are you in hiding? Have you pulled back from the battle to tend to your wounds? Sometimes we give up when the fight seems too hard. We mope and get accustomed to defeat.

> Therefore please hear this, you afflicted,
> And drunk but not with wine.
> Thus says your Lord,
> The LORD and your God,
> Who pleads the cause of His people:
> "See, I have taken out of your hand
> The cup of trembling,
> The dregs of the cup of My fury;
> You shall no longer drink it.
> But I will put it into the hand of those who afflict you,
> Who have said to you,
> 'Lie down, that we may walk over you.'
> And you have laid your body like the ground,
> And as the street, for those who walk over."
> (Isaiah 51:21–23)

In this passage the enemy says in effect, "Just give up so we can trample you." And what is the people's response? They did it! This is not the response that God wants us to have when our enemies seek to trample on us.

HOPE IN TROUBLED TIMES

While David was in the cave, he could look back on about forty years of war and remember crushing defeats, betrayals, scary moments, and crises of every variety. But he had also experienced great victories.

On the next two lines, write down some of your most notable victories. Has God helped you shake an addiction to a particular sin? Given you victory over depression, anxiety, worry, or fear? Answered long-carried burdens of repeated prayers? Brought back a loved one from destruction? Healed a broken body? Listened to your cry and responded?

_____

_____

In difficult circumstances, we must never lose sight of the times in our past when God has proven Himself trustworthy and faithful and more than able to deliver us from our enemies. The Bible encourages us to turn to God in troubling times. God is in control, and He is our hope. Ultimate victory belongs to God's people.

Psalm 43:1–2, 5

_____

_____

The King's Desire

As we saw above, David said with longing, "Oh, that someone would give me a drink of the water from the well of Bethlehem, which is by the gate!" The king was hot, thirsty, and tired. He was getting old, and most of his life had been spent at war. In fact, God wouldn't let David build the temple, because the king's life had been filled with so much bloodshed (1 Chronicles 22:8).

King David had the right to give orders. He was the ruler of the land, and no one would dispute his choice to send soldiers into battle. But in this case he didn't command anyone to get him water from his favorite well. That would have seemed selfish and arrogant. After all, couldn't His Highness just drink regular water like everyone else?

David did, however, make his desire known to those around him. We don't know exactly what he was thinking. Maybe he was just musing about the carefree days of his childhood in Bethlehem, when life was simpler and a relaxed afternoon included a cold drink from that refreshing well. Or maybe he intended for the mighty men to overhear his recollection and be stirred into action. David may have planned that this provocation would begin a great war which would regain the conquered territories of his people.

Whatever David was thinking, the warriors heard his desire. And what did they do? The next verse tells us the story: "So the three mighty men broke through the camp of the Philistines, drew water from the well of Bethlehem that was by the gate, and took it and brought it to David" (2 Samuel 23:16).

Let's shift the application of this story from David to the three mighty men. Our goal is to recognize that God can make us like them, accomplishing great things for our King and being victorious in battle because He is on our side. Here's the big question for mighty warriors in training: Are we close enough to our King to know how He feels? Do we hear the desires of His heart? Are we quick to move to fulfill what He wants even without receiving direct orders? Or does the Lord have to drag us forward into His will for our lives?

Psalm 110:3

_____

_____

When God calls, how do you respond? Check the one that applies to you:

☐ Pretend you didn't hear.
☐ Wait until He asks you specifically, preferably in an audible voice.
☐ Wait for orders and threats before you start moving—and then move really slowly.

Hopefully you don't do any of the above, but we all struggle sometimes to respond to God's call. Our goal should be to say, "Yes, Lord," and get moving. Jesus said that obedience is the true measure of whether or not we are disciples and the true measure of whether or not we really love Him.

Luke 6:46

_____

_____

John 14:15

_____

_____

True Story

1 Corinthians 1:26–29: For you see your calling, brethren, that not many wise according to the flesh, not many mighty, not many noble, are called. But God has chosen the foolish things of the world to put to shame the wise, and God has chosen the weak things of the world to put to shame the things which are mighty; and the base things of the world and the things which are despised God has chosen, and the things which are not, to bring to nothing the things that are, that no flesh should glory in His presence.

The Indian Tata SUV bounced along the dirt road on the way to a remote Gawali tribal village. We were waiting to begin the church service until the men returned from the fields after a hard day's work. Gradually about thirty people, leaving their sandals outside, filled the larger of the two rooms in the pastor's house. The other room contained only one bed and a small propane stove. Electric lines came into the poor, primitive village, but there was no power at the pastor's house. The men wired a small bulb to the SUV's battery and stuck it through the window. Enthusiastic worship with a tambourine filled the room, loud enough for all the neighbors to hear.

Our pastor friends each lead about six churches. The pastors visit each village and hold a service once a week, so "Sunday" for the villagers may be any day. Once the pastors have trained a pastor from within the church, they can leave it in his hands and go to the next village that doesn't have a church. There are three thousand villages without a church in the Yavatmal district alone—and that's just one county in one state of this huge country.

Each time I taught the Bible in one of these churches, I felt such a rush of joy and awe. It was like going back to the first-century church. Simple people with simple lives and a simple faith in God. No technology and no need for it. These were people who could relate perfectly to Jesus' parables about sowers, seeds, sheep, and fish.

Their prayers were loud and strong, with their hands lifted into the air, knowing that their hope was in heaven, not on the earth. Their testimonies included that of a formerly Hindu woman whose friend had suggested that she pray to Jesus to heal her daughter, who had been very sick for a long time. The woman said she had been to many gurus and made many sacrifices to the idols, but nothing had helped until she prayed to Jesus. Then her daughter started to get well, and this mother gave her life to the Lord.

God is present in this and countless small village churches around the world. Other villages are still waiting to hear the good news of Jesus Christ.

Sometimes we carry over the way that we relate to our parents into our walk with the Lord. Picture this scene as little Billy plays video games.

"Billy, would you take out the trash, please?'

"Unghrhm."

"Billy, it's stinking up the whole kitchen."

"Yeah, OK, Mom . . ."

"Billy, it's been ten minutes, and you still haven't moved!"

"Just a few more minutes so I can beat this level."

"WILLIAM FRANKLIN JACKSON, IF YOU DON'T GET UP THIS SECOND, I'M GOING TO COME OVER THERE AND—"

"OK, Mom, OK! I was coming! You don't have to get all mad!"

How much does it take for God to get us moving?

The Power of Obedience

Imagine the three warriors fighting through the Philistine guards, knowing that there were plenty of enemy troops in reserve, and trying not to spill the water they had taken. Picture one hand skillfully wielding a sword while the other pulled up a rope with a bucket on the end. Visualize the confusion of the Philistines as they realize that the three mighty men are not there to conquer the city, plunder the treasures, or take prisoners. They just want a jug of water.

What were these crazy Israelites up to, anyway? If only three warriors could break in, killing soldiers along the way, and then take water and leave alive, what did that mean for Philistine pride and confidence? The enemy would be deeply shaken.

The Philistines didn't seem to have very good memories, or maybe they were cocky and overconfident. Just a few chapters earlier, Jonathan had beaten a troop of Philistines with the help of only his young assistant, because he recognized that victory did not lie in skill or numbers but in God's intervention. "It may be that the Lord will work for us," he said. "For nothing restrains the Lord from saving by many or by few" (1 Samuel 14:6).

Recall that the three great heroes, years before this Bethlehem incident took place, had become such examples only after they had faced certain death for their king and had seen God come through. This happens all through the Old Testament: impossible odds mean nothing when God is in the picture.

Take, for example, King Jehoshaphat, when the armies of the Moabites, Ammonites, and Mount Seir surrounded his people.

2 Chronicles 20:12

_____

_____

2 Chronicles 20:15

_____

_____

In this case, God told them not to fight but to praise Him, and He promised He would come. As they did, the enemy armies turned against each other and fought until no one was left. What a principle to demoralize the devil! God comes to the aid of His people when they obey Him.

LIVING FOR GOD'S PURPOSES

God created you for a purpose that's much higher than just fitting in, getting an education, getting married, having kids, making money, and retiring to play golf in Florida. None of those things are bad in themselves, but they do not necessarily make a complete and purposeful life. For that, you need to find out from God why you're here. No one else can tell you. You can go through the motions all your life and then die and get to heaven before you find out that you may have missed it.

People who want to excel in any area know that sacrifice is required. Companies expect extra hours, work taken home on weekends, and total commitment from rising executives and potential salespeople of the year. Then they reward these sacrifices with money and perks. Do we live to serve a higher cause? Can we choose to make sacrifices when the rewards won't even show up in this lifetime?

When the mighty men brought the water from Bethlehem back to David, what did he do? Did David thank them profusely? Did he give them medals in a ceremony before all of the army? No! He wouldn't drink it, but poured out the water on the ground, offering it to the Lord. He said, "Far be it from me, O Lord, that I should do this! Is this not the blood of the men who went in jeopardy of their lives?" (2 Samuel 23:17). That water suddenly had a value beyond all other pitchers filled with liquid because the risk to the mighty men had been so great. King David felt unworthy to receive the water he had desired. He realized that only God deserves such a sacrifice.

Devotion to their king made the warriors willing to risk their lives to please him. Likewise, our sacrifices make the things we do for the Lord valuable in His sight. What God wants may not seem very important to people who see through natural instead of spiritual eyes. It's likely that every doctor or nurse tending the poor in the inner city or out in the bush has had skeptics shake their heads and wonder why they aren't in a comfortable practice in a nice office, making the big bucks. Some of God's warriors hear the call in midlife to leave careers before the payoff of secular success has fully come, and go into ministry for a fraction of their former salaries. Teachers who leave the comforts of suburbia for the ghetto or Ghana also rate a place in the category of the sacrificial.

How did these three mighty men become so loyal and dedicated that they would be willing to make such a sacrifice? Remember from the last chapter how they started. They were just faces in a crowd until their choices distinguished them from everyone else. It doesn't matter how you began. If the devil has ever told you that you'll never amount to anything in God's kingdom, that you're an unimportant nobody, here's hope. The important thing is that you stay loyal to your King. Fight the battles He sends your way, and your wisdom and skills will increase. The level of assignments from your King will also increase, in both risk and significance. Soon others will look to you, and you'll be recognized as a tested and proven warrior.

Philippians 2:13

_____

_____

The warriors didn't go grumbling about that self-centered, egomaniacal king who had to get what he wanted. Their love and devotion to David was so great that even this potential suicide mission didn't seem too big. In the same way, God works in our lives so that first we desire to do His will and then He works through us so that we are able to carry out His will. If you ask any of God's humble servants who have accomplished great deeds for the kingdom how they feel about it, they will say they are amazed that God could do so much through such an imperfect vessel.

Volunteer educator for children and adults overseas. Preferably someone with vision to break the cycle of poverty, train future leaders, and instill Christian foundations in families and communities.

According to the United Nations,

- 67 million primary-school-age children do not attend school;
- 53 percent of these are girls and 43 percent are in sub-Saharan Africa;
- 40 percent of children are kept out of school because of armed conflict; and
- 17 percent of the world's adults, or 793 million people, are illiterate, two-thirds of them women.

While working in a midwifery clinic in the Philippines, I (Kristin) decided to volunteer with people living in a garbage dump. The first day, I expected to see a few children playing in some trash but was shocked by what I saw instead: five thousand families, equaling thirty-two thousand people, living in a garbage dump that stretches two miles long and thirty feet high. Everywhere I looked were naked children of all ages, digging through trash, sleeping, and eating leftover McDonald's food and rice they found buried in the garbage. Everything was soaked because of

jungle rains and molding from days of balmy heat. The children made games of sliding through hand-made ditches in the garbage, their bodies plastered with mud and trash. I loved those kids. After a few wild games of duck-duck-goose, I decided to go back every week.

On my third visit, I met thirteen-year-old Mai-mai. I found out that she works full-time, seven hours a day, scavenging through trash and hoping to sell whatever she can find. A few years ago, her younger brother helped, but one day while he was sleeping in a heap of trash, a garbage-truck operator unknowingly lifted the pile and took it to another city. Mai-mai hasn't seen him since and assumes he's dead, buried underneath mountains of trash. Now Mai-mai works to survive.

We talked about her dreams for the future. This wasn't easy for her—a stark contrast to every American child's shouts of becoming a doctor or ballerina. Eventually Mai-mai smiled and said, "I know. I want a cell phone." This affected me strongly; Mai-mai had no aspirations for her future. I told her that she could buy a cell phone, but she had to go to school so that she could get a job, so she could make purchases. Mai-mai smiled again, a smile that pitied me, the poor American foreigner who knew nothing. She reminded me that school takes place during the day, the time she has to work. School is in a distant building, requiring money for transportation. School uniforms cost fifty pesos (roughly one American dollar), which she did not have.

My eyes widened to the panoramic view in front of me, and a reality I had been avoiding finally

sank its teeth deep inside. I saw young mothers with newborns, boils on their foreheads from clogged pores. I saw children digging through trash—rotten goat meat, flies, condoms—looking for something to sell, something to eat. I saw elderly, using the bag-and-throw method of disposing bodily waste. I understood it then: street people are born on the streets, raised on the streets, have their own kids on the streets, and die on the streets. Without prevention or intervention, most people do not have tools to uproot themselves from the cycle of poverty.

The need for education around the world provides an incredible opportunity for Christians. Countries that are both open and closed to the gospel are searching for volunteers to help their people. But simply teaching kids math and reading is not enough. By purposefully incorporating the gospel and biblical wisdom into classrooms, Christians can make a practical difference in the lives of hundreds of children while affecting generations to come through the message of salvation. If you've received any education, you are a candidate for teaching others overseas. Ask the Lord if you should volunteer your education today to make an impact in a community forever.

It's your world—do something today!

Ask local schools if they have an after-school program for children in the neighborhood. Volunteer with a few of your friends and build relationships through tutoring and sharing the good news of Jesus. Also look into Child Evangelism Fellowship: *www.cefonline.com*.

Luke 17:10

_____

_____

Isaiah 45:3

_____

_____

Is there something in a village that your King wants? Does He see something of great value in a place under the control of the enemy?

Villages come in many different varieties. Some are reachable only after days of river travel, unless you happen to have a helicopter. In an era of speedy transportation, we forget that technology has yet to reach everyone. At a recent King's Kids leadership conference in Shanghai, some of our workers traveled up to six days to get there. There are still nearly inaccessible places where people have never heard the name of Jesus. Other places may be easier to get to physically but are just as or more difficult to reach because of government restrictions. Your destiny may include a tamer lifestyle based in the affluent West, with your service to God and obedience never putting you in the risky situations of the three mighty warriors. That's fine. But just suppose that someone reading this (and why couldn't it be you?) has a destiny in the eternal plans of God to take on the giants, win back the land, defeat the enemies, and satisfy the longing of a King. God is looking with longing at Saudi Arabia, North Korea, and other places where millions of people are in need of Him. Could you have a part in serving them and retrieving them for the Lord?

Not only villages but whole cities and nations are under the enemy's control, and the King wants them back. Large parts of the planet serve idols and worship nature. The names of false gods are still on the lips of millions of devoted but deluded worshipers. Every person and every part of the world belongs to God, but the enemy has gone to great lengths to take them captive.

Psalm 24:1

_____

_____

1 John 5:19

_____

_____

From the tiny Maldive Islands to vast China, God wants His land back. He sees treasure where others see only trouble. He sees spiritual needs where others see only business opportunities and new markets for products. Above all other things, God desires the hearts of those who don't know Him. They are made in His image and are of the greatest value to Him.

Have you ever had to buy a gift for someone who can afford whatever he or she wants? What do you get for the person who already has everything? In the same way, what do you give to God, who owns everything in the whole world?

Isaiah 66:1–2

_____

_____

God desires one thing: people who will love and serve Him and take His word seriously. Will you be one of those?

Wrap-up

Let's wrap this up and apply it to our own lives. Let's put the teachings into a fresh prayer that sums up all we have seen in this chapter.

Father, if You can make a mighty warrior out of me, then I'm willing. I don't know how You could accomplish much through me, with my weaknesses and struggles. I really do want to be close enough to You to hear what's on Your heart, and I want to be quick to obey. It's easy to promise that, but following through is a lot harder. Help me, Lord! Please show me the things that are important to You, and help me have the faith to believe You really will be with me when I step out to do Your will. In Jesus' name. Amen.

What stands out to you in this prayer?

_____

_____

How will you put it into practice?

_____

_____

What has God been saying to you this week?

_____

_____

How does this affect your daily life?

_____

_____

How does this affect your life plans?

_____

_____

SCRIPTURE MEMORY

Psalm 2:8
Ask of Me, and I will give You
The nations for Your
    inheritance,
And the ends of the earth for
    Your possession.

Psalm 111:6
He has declared to His people
    the power of His works,
In giving them the heritage of
    the nations.

DAILY BIBLE READING

✓ Check when completed

Sunday	Ezekiel 16–19
Monday	Ezekiel 20–24
Tuesday	Ezekiel 25–28
Wednesday	Ezekiel 29–32
Thursday	Ezekiel 33–36
Friday	Ezekiel 37–39
Saturday	Ezekiel 40–43

BIBLE READING QUESTIONS/THOUGHTS

_____
_____
_____
_____
_____
_____
_____
_____
_____
_____
_____

PRAYER NEEDS THIS WEEK

_____
_____
_____
_____
_____
_____
_____
_____
_____
_____

8

RECEIVING YOUR INHERITANCE

I magine one day a distant relative who always liked you passes away and suddenly your whole financial status changes. Something like this happened to a man in my church back in the late 1980s. His mother died, and his life changed dramatically. With one huge check he paid off the mortgage for the entire addition to the church building. Then he bought an airplane, moved away, and hopefully lived happily ever after. All of us benefited from his blessing.

Or imagine you win "Who Wants to Be a Millionaire?" or the lottery. Now all of your expenses are paid, and you will never have any financial stress again. Have you ever thought about something amazing like that happening to you?

The idea of receiving an inheritance and having our lives change dramatically appeals to us. An inheritance is something you receive when someone dies. But if you don't know about the person's will, if someone never tells you what was left to you, you could miss out on it completely.

The Bible has a lot to say about inheritances. Our question today is, What did Jesus leave us when He died? What did He leave us in His will? God has left us much more than many of us have the vision to obtain.

Romans 8:17

_____

_____

Ephesians 1:11

_____

_____

There's a story told of a slave in the Deep South before the Civil War. He had a good master, and after slavery was abolished, he stayed on and worked faithfully for him. The master died and left the entire plantation to this former slave, who was now an old man himself. When the lawyers called him in to explain his good fortune, they couldn't get him to understand that the place where he had always worked was now his own property. He just couldn't imagine that. They told him he was now a wealthy man and that he could have all that his former master had left behind. After thinking a while, he asked, "Do you think that I could have as much as five dollars?" They said yes and much more. He replied, "No, I think five dollars will do." So they gave him five dollars, and he went back to work on the plantation, not realizing that it was now _his_ plantation.

He couldn't think big enough to collect his inheritance. Can we think big enough to collect ours?

WHOSE WORLD IS THIS, ANYWAY?

It's God's world. He created it, and it still belongs to Him. Although the world system fell with Adam and is under the control of the kingdom of darkness, the planet and the people belong to God. It's up to the church to proclaim His right to rule here. It's our job to recapture the nations from the usurper, Satan, and see Jesus take His rightful place as Lord over everything.

Colossians 1:14–16

_____

_____

_____

_____

In the Father's will, Jesus will be exalted over all the earth. God has given Jesus dominion over all the nations, and as joint heirs with Christ, we can ask God for the nations and He will give them to us.

Psalm 2:8

_____

_____

_____

Psalm 111:6

_____

_____

_____

_____

Nations! Not just an inheritance of a house or a car or land. Not just a family business or even millions of dollars. None of that small stuff. God has given us an inheritance of nations.

But what does that mean, exactly? Obviously not that we own nations or that we rule over them. It means that we can capture nations for the kingdom of God. It means that we can defeat the works of the devil that blind nations in their sins and deliver their inhabitants from bondage. It means that we can change the course of history!

THE HERITAGE OF THE SERVANTS OF THE LORD

Why should we bother with a lost world when there are so many pressing problems so close to home?

Because over a billion Muslims bow before Allah five times each day, and he's not God.

True Story

"We are not worth much. Why do you play with us?"

The street children in the Philippines are poor, especially the ones whose parents can't afford to send them to school. They roam the streets while their parents try to find ways to put rice on the table. An example of this level of poverty is the young couple we met on the street, about to have their first baby. The Christian maternity clinic asked them for a nominal two-dollar fee for all the care the woman would receive, including delivery. Her husband rides a bike through Cebu every day, scrounging for something to recycle or sell, but couldn't come up with two dollars, so the clinic waived the fees for them.

These street kids eagerly met our team each day when we held evangelistic meetings, came by the clinic for lunch, or stopped there between Vacation Bible Schools. One day a little girl surprised us with the quote above. I wonder who lied to this little girl and others like her, saying they were not worth much. Maybe they are illiterate and ragged. Maybe they suffer from malnutrition and will never get an education. Sadly, some will end up in the sex trade and become prostitutes, but they are definitely not worthless.

Our time playing with these children, praying with them, and presenting the message of Jesus was an example of a far greater love than our own. Though we were only in that location for two weeks, it was enough time to make a lasting impression. We saw this repeatedly as people remembered us by name from the previous year or asked for those who had come the previous year. Our message was designed to point them to One who promised to never leave or forsake them if they would believe on Him. Even grubby little street children are of infinite value to God.

Allah teaches his followers to conquer the entire world with bloodshed, as opposed to Jesus' message of forgiveness of sins and new life.

Because nearly a billion Hindus honor the elephant god, the monkey god, and the snake god, and this dishonors the true and living God. The carved stone idols have no power to answer prayer, comfort the sorrowful, or provide for the needs of the poor.

Because another billion Asians live in fear of their dead ancestors, revere Buddha, and make sacrifices to the spirits. Superstitions and philosophies cannot bring peace to their hearts.

Because 80–90 percent of the world's children are growing up in non-Christian homes. They don't have parents who will aim them toward having a personal relationship with Jesus, living a godly life, or avoiding the pitfalls of materialism and temptation.

Because last year twenty-two million Catholics made pilgrimages to the shrine of the Virgin of Guadalupe, and she's not God either. Although Mary's obedience is a great example to believers (Luke 1:38), she was a sinner who needed a Savior just like the rest of us (Luke 1:46–47).

Isaiah 54:17

_____

_____

Psalm 149:6–9

_____

_____

We are all a part of the biggest thing happening in the earth—the reason that all creation was created and that the earth continues to spin around the sun. It's the advancing kingdom of God. I'm not content to be a spectator. I won't be satisfied hearing others' stories of victories. But to be world changers and history makers takes vision, and I think sometimes ours is limited. We are so preoccupied with the immediate that we forget the eternal. We're busy with the small world of our own personal lives and problems, and we lose sight of the bigger picture.

Have you seen *A Bug's Life* or *Antz*? The same theme runs through both movies. There's love, romance, intrigue, suspense, conflict, danger, all in a few square inches! From time to time the camera zooms back so we can see it's all happening in a tiny corner of this huge world, but to the ants, that's all there is. Their universe is a few yards square.

I'm afraid that unless God shows us the bigger picture, we will live like ants. Getting beyond the ant stage means fresh vision and God's revision of our priorities. He will have to take away the world's value system because it blinds us to what is real. For us to receive the inheritance of what Jesus has left us means change.

A Tragedy . . . or a Victory?

A young missionary died of meningitis in Cairo, Egypt. Bill's coworkers were impressed by his humility and eagerness to win others to the Lord. Bill passed out gospel tracts in the blistering Egyptian heat, refusing to pamper himself, since his sole desire in life was to be a missionary. He was only twenty-five years old.

Befriender of future leaders for the next generation. Must be willing to share friendship, fellowship, and hope with college students and surrogate families.

The college campus is ripe for harvest. Every year, thousands of young people enter this experience looking for new friends, exploring new philosophies, and searching for something to do with their futures. Eventually, these college freshmen become the leading businessmen, politicians, teachers, and parents who direct society and shape values. Furthermore, there are hundreds of thousands of foreign students coming to American universities every year. They need people to teach them English and culture, but more than anything, they need relationships. The college campus represents an ideal opportunity to be a witness for Jesus—where else will you find thousands of young people, unsure of what to do with their lives, waiting for someone to give them direction?

Unfortunately, many Christians feel as if the college campus is a lost cause, as they must combat secular ideals, professors who openly criticize faith, and nonstop temptation to live the party lifestyle. Yet there is no area on earth that isn't subject to the authority of Jesus. The college campus is in dire need of the love and hope of Christ, as US statistics show:

- 30 percent of students have felt such intense depression that they had difficulty functioning.
- 25 percent of college women have used an eating disorder to manage weight.
- 40 percent of foreign students say they have no American friends.
- The second leading cause of death among college students is suicide.

In the midst of a dark place, Christians must let their lights shine brightly, trusting that Jesus does not let His word return void.

At Texas State University, football player Shadrick Bell labeled himself a Christian but placed all his hope in football, fame, and education. Yet in his junior year, a campus missionary reached out to him, inviting him to church and telling him about victory in Jesus. Shad committed his heart to God and found more than initial self-worth; he found the call to love God wholeheartedly and serve Him forever. Shad soon began a Bible study. It started small, but within one year, over fifty men were attending. Working alongside his college ministry and church, Shad raised up another leader and divided the group in half. The groups have continued to grow, and there are now seven men's college groups with fourteen men in training to be small-group leaders. After getting his master's degree, Shad turned down a job offer with a major sporting goods company and instead chose to be a campus missionary through Every Nation Campus Ministries. You can find him today at Texas State University, interrupting students' lives and sharing the hope of Christ.

It's your world—do something today!

Ask your family to "adopt" a college student. Once a week, have that student (and his or her friends) over for a home-cooked meal, board games or movies, and a Bible study. Additionally, pray about supporting a campus missionary. Find a ministry on your campus (Every Nation Campus Ministries, Cru, the Navigators, IVCF, BSM, etc.) and partner financially with someone who works full-time spreading the gospel on campus.

Reach out to foreign students on your local college campus. Introduce them to the gospel, and you could be training future missionaries! When they go back to their native countries, they can explain salvation to their families and friends.

Does the word *tragic* come to mind? Was Bill's life well spent or wasted? He graduated from Yale University and could have done well in life. When he died, Bill didn't even own a car. Was he a success or a failure? That depends on whether you look at his life from the world's perspective or the Lord's perspective. Do you see things based on time or eternity?

Would your opinion of Bill change if you knew that his last name was Borden? As in Borden dairy products. He was the heir to a vast fortune, but he gave it away to various Christian organizations and went to a backward country and an early grave. Was he a fool? On earth it's easy for most people to say that he wasted his life, that he blew his chance at happiness and fulfillment. But where are happiness and fulfillment found? Bill's friends would say he found them in the slums of Cairo. What was the common opinion in heaven on the day Bill arrived? Do they count him as a loser there? When Bill stood before the One he served, do you think he was embarrassed at the way he had lived or ready to face the Master?

I want a piece of the action—how about you?

True Story

The man in the picture with me is the sheikh who leads the Yezidi people. The Yezidis are devil worshippers. Almost one million Yezidis live in the Kurdish region of the Middle East, which includes parts of Iran, Iraq, Turkey, Syria, and Armenia. They believe that there is a Creator but that he is far away from us and put seven angels in charge of various things. Satan is the angel in charge of earth. (Sounds a little like 2 Corinthians 4:4!) They call him the Peacock Angel, the proud one (like Isaiah 14:12–15).

They are the only religion that formally worships Satan but believes he has repented and has been forgiven and restored. It was intimidating to think of going to the village of Lalish, where their main temple is located, but we committed to take an Egyptian church planter who has targeted the Yezidi and is moving there with his family. On what happened to be my birthday, we drove through beautiful mountains and passed through two checkpoints of heavily armed freedom fighters. The village is located in a canyon with a stream from which they believe the flood of Noah's day began.

Tourists are welcome to see the temple and village. We entered and immediately noted that everyone in the village was barefoot. I have strong convictions against taking off my shoes in a religious setting, because it is the universal sign of respect for a god, going back to Moses and the burning bush. Every Hindu or Buddhist temple and Islamic mosque requires worshipers to take off their shoes. I've seen firsthand the demonic powers in these places and told the other three men in our group that I wouldn't take my shoes off in the village. They didn't feel the same convictions and left their shoes behind to tour the temple, where they saw the black snake idol (which Yezidis believe protected the ark during the flood), the burnt offerings, and the sacred pillars. I kept watching and waiting for signs of demonization but never saw any.

While I was waiting outside the temple, groups of kids gathered around. They asked my religion, and I answered that I follow Isa al-Masih according to the way of the Injil. In Arabic this means I follow Jesus the Messiah according to the New Testament. Some spoke a few words of English, limited to "action movies" and "Angelina Jolie." It's funny how our culture spreads to the most remote places on earth! Then a group of very serious young men gathered around me and said, "You must take off your shoes." I smiled and said that I wasn't going into their temple, as I backed toward the street. They were not happy about this but didn't pursue me.

I realized that we didn't know the taboos in this culture or the consequences of breaking them. Sure enough, the others had unknowingly stepped on the threshold of the doorway between rooms in the temple, which caused an uproar. A few minutes later more young men replaced the curious children and teenagers who were standing around me and said, "You *must* take off your shoes." I made the same excuse, but one interrupted, "This is a sacred place. TAKE OFF YOUR SHOES!" I knew this could get ugly fast. *What am I doing here alone?* I thought. I backed away from the angry young men, not taking my eyes off them but realizing that we were a long way from help. They didn't pursue me, and the Lord watched out for me.

Soon the rest of our small group arrived, and a young man the others had met invited us to eat lunch with his family. Personally, I was ready to leave, but it was important for the church planter to make these contacts.

I wondered what would happen if they said grace to the devil before our meal. My concern was that the Lord might require me to say something that wouldn't go over well with our hosts, but I knew that if He commanded me to speak, I would have no choice. My level of stress was rising. Violations of honor are a big enough offense in the Middle East without telling your hosts that they blaspheme the living God by honoring His enemy. Thankfully, there was no prayer, and we had a great feast for my birthday lunch.

Next, we were expected to stay for baptisms. This is the only place in the world where children can be baptized into the Yezidi faith, and we happened to show up on a day for baptisms. The idea of watching children essentially being dedicated to Satan caused me to shudder, and once again I wondered what the Lord might require me to say. We certainly couldn't congratulate them or join in any religious festivities.

It turned out that we would have had to wait for a long time until the ceremony, so we graciously excused ourselves to drive several hours back to the Iraqi city where we were staying. Our mission of helping the church planter make contact was a success, and he had new friends among the Yezidis. This was my second most exciting birthday ever—second only to being surrounded by the enraged mob with machetes in Haiti!

1 John 2:28

_____

_____

Revelation 22:12

_____

_____

What kind of reward awaits us in eternity? In the time we have left on earth—and we never know how long that will be—what will we do in obedience to God that we will be able to show Him when He asks us to give an account for our lives?

Bill's story happened in 1913. A hundred years later, we're still reading and talking about this incredible self-sacrifice, this incredible clarity of vision, trading the temporary for the eternal. In a hundred years, will anyone be talking about you or me? What if your life became one that was recorded in biographies to inspire generations to come? What if you made choices so radical that your story inspired people whose grandparents haven't been born yet to do great things for God? What if . . .

How Did He Get There?

You may wonder how Bill got there, spiritually speaking. An article titled "Freshman Bill Borden" in *The Yale Standard* (Fall 1970, p. 6), quoting from the book *Borden of Yale* by Mrs. Howard Taylor, gives this background:

"He came to college far ahead, spiritually, of any of us. He had already given his heart in full surrender to Christ and had really done it. We who were his classmates learned to lean on him and find in him a strength that was solid as a rock, just because of this settled purpose and consecration." . . .

During his first semester at Yale, Bill started the movement that transformed the campus. His friend wrote: "It was well on in the first term when Bill and I began to pray together in the morning before breakfast . . . a third student joined us and soon after a fourth. . . ."

Borden's group was the beginning of the daily groups for prayer that spread to every one of the college classes. By the end of Bill's first year, 150 freshmen had become interested in meeting for weekly Bible studies. By the time he was a senior, 1,000 out of the 1,300 students were meeting in groups like these.

Bill made it his habit to choose the most "incorrigible" students and bring them to salvation. In his sophomore year we organized Bible-study groups and divided up the class of three hundred or more, each man interested taking a certain number, so that all might, if possible, be reached. The names were gone over one by one, and the question asked, "Who will take this person or that?" When it came to one who was a hard proposition there would be an ominous pause. Nobody wanted the responsibility. Then Bill's voice would be heard: "Put him down to me."

Bill Borden did not confine his work to Yale. He rescued drunks on the streets of New Haven and founded the Yale Hope Mission to rehabilitate them. "He might often be found in the lower parts of the city at night—on the street, in a cheap lodging house or some restaurant to which he had taken a poor hungry fellow to feed him—seeking to lead men to Christ."

. . . [One of his classmates said]: "He certainly was one of the strongest characters I have ever known, and he put backbone into the rest of us at college. There was real iron in him, and I always felt he was of the stuff martyrs were made of, and heroic missionaries of more modern times."

Although he was a millionaire, Bill "seemed to realize always that he must be about his Father's business, and not wasting time in the pursuit of amusement."

Think about the inscription on Borden's grave. After describing his love and sacrifices for the kingdom of God and for Muslim people, it said: "Apart from faith in Christ, there is no explanation for such a life."

Here's the point: Bill Borden looked for ways to serve the Lord in his immediate setting. He was faithful in little things, and God gave him greater responsibilities. This principle works for us too.

Luke 16:10–13

Don't Be Sluggish!
Hebrews 6:11–12

Many churches put up flags in the sanctuary, showing places their missionaries are serving. If your church does this, which nations will have a flag on the wall showing that you went to claim your inheritance there? Where will you make your mark on this world for the kingdom of God?

What did Jesus leave you in His will? Picture yourself following in the footsteps of those who have been world changers before you—people who went through the same struggles you face, pressed on with God, and found their destinies. They weren't super-Christians. They were just regular believers who chose to make a difference. You can be one too.

Revelation 17:14

_____

_____

Will we live like ants, our lives consumed by the pressing concerns of our own tiny world, or will we—as individuals and as a church—catch a bigger, eternal vision?

Pray, Give, or Go

There are three ways we can receive our inheritance of the nations:

Pray. We used to visit a nursing home every Saturday with our youth group. I made friends with an elderly Christian woman, Mrs. Grace Hecker, who had taught Sunday school for countless years in the Baptist church. She would sit in her wheelchair, wrinkled hands folded over a Bible. One day I asked her if she didn't get bored, sitting there every day. I'll never forget her response. "Oh, no! I can always think of another missionary to pray for." I am so grateful for the people who pray for our ministry. Whose ministry do you pray for?

Give. In previous wars, the military discovered it takes about eleven soldiers working behind the scenes for every one on the front lines. A jet fighter requires about 450 people in its support crew. If you're called to stay—and obviously by these numbers most Christians will be called to stay—you still have an active part in the Great Commission. Many Christians think their budget is too tight to give, but our budgets reflect our priorities!

Go. Don't think you're not eligible.

I suggest we do all three. Pray, give, _and_ go. You and I can't be everywhere, but we can pray for God's kingdom to come everywhere. Sometimes I hear about people getting opportunities that God hasn't given to me. I can give to those people. And there are many places I can actually go. So can you. Are you receiving your inheritance?

Daydreams

What do you daydream about? When the classroom is hot and Mr. or Mrs. Boring is droning on endlessly, where does your mind go? Thoughts of the opposite sex? Understandable—and fine as long as they are rated PG. Travel, adventure, and new experiences? Maybe God put that dream there. But if your daydreams revolve around getting more things, obtaining money and power, or gaining more status in the eyes of others, you need a reality check.

Psalm 19:14

_____

_____

Too many Christians have had their values hijacked by the world. Is your overriding pursuit self-focused or kingdom-focused? Maybe one way to see is to think about receiving a huge earthly inheritance. Some long-forgotten relative remembered you and left you an unbelievable fortune. What are the thoughts that come to mind? Lavish spending on everything from your daydreams—sports cars, clothes, mansions, and vacations? Incredible presents for all your friends? Never having to work again? Or do your thoughts turn to the good you could do with this fortune—people you could help, hungry children to feed, missionaries going out, medical clinics in remote places, Bibles to print, churches and schools to build, ministries to support in the far corners of the earth?

Luke 12:15–21

_____

_____

Luke 12:34

_____

_____

The average earthly inheritance is wasted and gone in a year or two. The average heavenly inheritance is eternal. Our questions today are, What did Jesus leave us when He died? What did He leave us in His will? And will we receive our inheritance of the nations?

WRAP-UP

Let's wrap this up and apply it to our own lives. Let's put the illustration of inheritance into a fresh prayer that sums up all we have seen this week.

Lord, don't let me live for anything smaller than Your purpose for my life. Keep me from wasting the limited number of days You have given me. Don't let me live like an ant or a slug. Show me Your vision for my life, beginning right now. Let me see as clearly as Bill Borden! Let my life bring glory to You! In Jesus' name. Amen.

What stands out to you in this prayer?

_____

_____

How will you put it into practice?

_____

_____

What has God been saying to you this week?

_____

_____

How does this affect your daily life?

_____

_____

How does this affect your life plans?

_____

_____

SCRIPTURE MEMORY

1 John 2:15
Do not love the world or the things in the world. If anyone loves the world, the love of the Father is not in him.

Revelation 5:9
And they sang a new song, saying:

"You are worthy to take the
    scroll,
And to open its seals;
For You were slain,
And have redeemed us to
    God by Your blood
Out of every tribe and tongue
    and people and nation."

FINISH READING YOUR BOOK AND COMPLETE BOOK REPORT 2 ON THE NEXT PAGE.

DAILY BIBLE READING

✓ Check when completed

Sunday	Ezekiel 44–48
Monday	Daniel 1–3
Tuesday	Daniel 4–6
Wednesday	Daniel 7–9
Thursday	Daniel 10–12
Friday	Hosea 1–3
Saturday	Hosea 4–6

BIBLE READING QUESTIONS/THOUGHTS

_____
_____
_____
_____
_____
_____
_____
_____
_____
_____
_____

PRAYER NEEDS THIS WEEK

_____
_____
_____
_____
_____
_____
_____
_____

9

BOOK REPORT 2

Book title: _____

Author: _____

What did you like about it?

_____
_____
_____
_____

Would you recommend it to others?

_____
_____

What impressed you most about this book?

_____
_____
_____
_____
_____

How did God use the book to speak to you?

_____
_____
_____
_____
_____

Other comments or thoughts about the book:

_____
_____
_____
_____
_____

Lesson nine

OBJECTIONS TO MISSIONS

Through thirty-two years of short-term missions with teenagers, I've heard many people object to missionary work. Let's take a look at the most common objections.

OBJECTION TO MISSIONS #1: THE LOST

"We have plenty of lost people in our own city." True, but most North American cities also have a large Christian witness. In my city we have twelve pages of churches in our phone book (though not all preach the gospel clearly), one Christian TV station and four Christian radio stations, six Christian bookstores, and numerous ministries that reach out to the homeless, truck drivers, businesspeople, youth, and other sectors of society. It's probably similar where you live, and those from bigger cities have even more spiritual resources available. The reasonable conclusion is that any spiritually hungry person in my city, or in yours, could find someone who could tell him or her how to find the Lord. If necessary, he or she could follow an SUV with a fish bumper sticker or stop someone in a "Got Jesus?" shirt or look for a WWJD bracelet or cross or dove earrings or tattoos of Moses crossing the Red Sea or . . .

Let's contrast that with a common scenario in central India. Everyone in Amol's village is Hindu. All the ancestors he can remember have been Hindu. There's not a single Bible in his language or a Christian who speaks it. He has never met a believer in Jesus or seen a church. His spiritual options include Ganesh the elephant god, Hanuman the monkey god, Nag the cobra god, Lakshmi the six-armed goddess, or blue-skinned Krishna. The concept of forgiveness is completely foreign to him. He expects to be punished severely in his next reincarnation for every mistake made in this life. The gods are too busy with their own lives to have any concern for him, unless he makes dramatic and costly sacrifices to gain their attention. Even then, they don't love him. Grace is unimaginable, and there's no hope in his life.

Revelation 7:9–10

_____

_____

Which of these two people—the person in my or your city, or Amol in central India—needs a gospel presentation more? Shouldn't we expect that the person with easy access to the gospel would be responsible under the grace of God to take initiative to seek Him? Doesn't it make sense to make the extra effort to reach out to those in non-Christian cultures who have not heard the gospel?

OBJECTION TO MISSIONS #2: THE POOR

"We have plenty of poor people right here in our city." True, but we have food stamps, welfare, job training programs, adult literacy classes, WIC (food supplied to Women, Infants, and Children), homeless shelters, and government hospitals. There are churches with benevolence budgets, community outreach ministries, help for the addicted, crisis pregnancy centers, and food banks.

Isaiah 58:6–11

_____

_____

Millions of foreign poor would love to be one of our homeless people. The difference is immense. Poor countries don't have a safety net to catch the desperate, and corrupt governments steal foreign aid that comes their way. That's why thirty-six thousand people literally starve to death every day, why babies die from diseases we've eradicated in North America, and why so many people overseas are crippled, deaf, or blind—because they don't have access to food and can't afford even basic medical care.

Ecclesiastes 4:1

_____

_____

Add to a lack of sufficient food dirty drinking water, parasites, no education, religious or cultural mistreatment of girls and women, oppressive and brutal police and soldiers, natural disasters . . . Life is harder there, and the poor are poorer there. Sure, we should help people close to home, and we do this continually in our city, but most people in our cities don't really know what true poverty is. Can you hear the cry of the poor?

Objection to Missions #3: The Cost

"Who's paying for all these mission trips? It's very expensive." You have permission to skip this section if you don't want to be challenged. It's not going to be pretty. We've ministered in nearly thirty churches in our city alone through the years. Every one of them could send lots of new missionaries. How do I know this? I call it the "SUV factor."

Several years ago, our Ethiopia trip cost about $90,000. People usually gasp when they hear such a high number. It cost that much for thirty-five people to fly to Africa and minister to the world's poorest nation for five weeks. Yes, $90,000 seems like a lot, but put that number into perspective. That's the cost of two SUVs. How many SUVs are parked at your church on Sunday?

In twenty years, those SUVs will be headed toward the junkyard. In twenty years, the people we led to the Lord in Ethiopia will be headed toward heaven and taking others with them. Which is the better use of money?

Let's make this as graphic as possible. Here are two SUVs worth about $90,000 total. Write $90,000 in the space next to the pictures.

Now look at the Ethiopian boy. Write the value of his soul next to his picture.

Couldn't do it? Of course not! Christians know a soul and a dollar amount can't be compared. (If you could put a dollar value on his soul, please call me so I can pray for you.)

One SUV is about the cost of keeping a family on the mission field for a year. Church parking lots are full of them. Don't you think that among us we could collectively make the small sacrifices to fund more workers to go to the nations? And if we don't, how will the American church answer to the Lord when He shows us how warped our priorities are?

Luke 12:48

_____

_____

_____

_____

Now, of course it is true that keeping a family on the mission field long-term is more cost effective than sending short-term teams. But even the relatively high cost of short-term missions is a worthwhile investment. Short-term missions have several significant benefits. They frequently involve young people who are free to adjust their education and career plans according to new understandings of God's call on their lives. They allow businesspeople to see firsthand what is happening on foreign fields and form partnerships for job creation and financial support. They bring fresh vision back to congregations that would otherwise feel disconnected from their missionaries. Short-term teams cause excitement in the churches that send them and create a group of people with outreach experience, which can be put to use on the local level as well as broadening the pool of future missionaries. But all of this requires money.

Let's get very blunt. The average born-again Christian adult in the United States gave total offerings of $1,641 in 2005. For some, that was a sacrifice. For others, it's a joke, not a tithe. About 95 percent of their giving was to ministry that benefited people in the US and less than 5 percent to reaching the rest of the world. If the people of God continue to give at the same level while using our finances to seek comforts and lavish lifestyles, we have effectively put a price tag on this little boy's soul, and millions like him. He is worth less to us than our own pleasures. Our status symbols matter more than his eternity. Keeping up with the neighbors and taking pride in our possessions, rather than the values of the kingdom, become our new benchmarks of real success.

1 John 2:15

_____

_____

Say either "amen!" or "ouch!"

If my assessment of the situation is wrong, I need to retract what I've said. If it's true—wouldn't you rather find out here than there? Doesn't it make sense to see from Scripture what we can expect on Judgment Day so we can be prepared when God asks us to render an account of our lives? Doesn't wisdom tell us that avoiding unpleasant surprises before God, when it's too late to do anything differently, is better than cultivating spiritual blindness by turning down the volume knob on our conscience and avoiding conviction because it's uncomfortable?

Revelation 5:9

_____

_____

This is not a poverty mentality—it's a priority mentality. It's not saying that Christians shouldn't have nice things or enjoy the fruits of their hard work. It's saying that we should determine where our priorities are and see whether they match the Lord's priorities. This is not saying that an individual family should shoulder an impossible burden, but that the body of Christ collectively, and each congregation, can do so much more if each individual and each family does their part.

2 Corinthians 8:13

_____

_____

Most of the people reading this are teenagers or college students. Your life and lifestyle lie ahead, and right now you're in a time when you're making decisions and setting a pattern for the next fifty to seventy years. Will you surpass my generation in dedication and sacrifice? Will your zeal for God be fueled by obedience and vision or quenched by falling into the traps that captured my generation?

REASONS PEOPLE OBJECT TO MISSIONS

We've examined three common objections to missions, but why do people even raise these and other objections to missions? I suspect fear that God could call them to go often drives them to invent reasons why it's not wise or necessary for anyone to go. I believe there are two significant and common reasons: (1) selfishness and (2) they haven't seen it for themselves. Let's look at these in more detail.

First, let's look at the most selfish man in the Bible. King Hezekiah had blown it badly. Just after God healed him from a fatal illness, he let the son of an enemy king come into his palace. Hezekiah boastfully showed off all his riches and the strength of his army, not realizing that the enemy prince was taking careful notes. It wasn't long before Hezekiah's kingdom fell to Babylon.

Then Isaiah said to Hezekiah, "Hear the word of the LORD of hosts: 'Behold, the days are coming when all that is in your house, and what your fathers have accumulated until this day, shall be carried to Babylon; nothing shall be left,' says the LORD. 'And they shall take away some of your sons who will descend from you, whom you will beget; and they shall be eunuchs in the palace of the king of Babylon.'"

So Hezekiah said to Isaiah, "The word of the LORD which you have spoken is good!" For he said, "At least there will be peace and truth in my days." (Isaiah 39:5–8)

Can you imagine a king or president, entrusted with the welfare of his people, who hears that they will be destroyed by the enemy in a few years and yet rejoices because it won't happen in his day? Can you imagine a father, hearing that his sons would be castrated and enslaved, is happy that it won't happen to him?

A look at Hezekiah's selfishness is also a challenge to look into our own hearts. Are you content, in a world full of pain, to simply avoid experiencing personal pain as much as possible? Or do you feel a God-given responsibility to do what you can for others in pain?

In his famous book *How Should We Then Live?*, theologian Francis Schaeffer points out that most Americans live for two false values: personal peace and affluence (or prosperity). As long as these two values aren't in danger, we will be happy. Are we any different from Hezekiah?

Is it enough that things go well for us personally? Is the basis for genuine contentment simply the fulfillment of our individual goals? A step beyond this level, and beyond Hezekiah's shortsightedness, is to care for the well-being of our family, and maybe our close friends. Beyond that, the easiest thing is to close our eyes to the rest of the world and pretend it's not there.

Have you ever heard that ostriches will bury their heads in the sand when danger approaches, thinking that then the predators won't be able to see them? That's actually a myth, but it illustrates our point. It's like a toddler who is

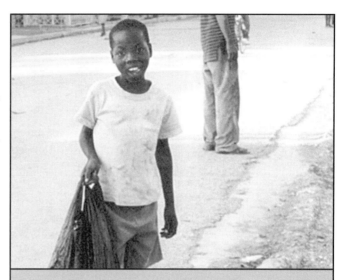

True Story

The need for missions even in unexpected places became clearer as we ministered on five Caribbean islands. A much-coveted destination for cruises and once-in-a-lifetime dream vacations, those beautiful islands need missionary work, leadership training, and outreaches to kids, even if it may have been hard for my supporters to understand why. It's difficult for those called to missions—whether short- or long-term—in destinations popular with tourists to convince the folks back home that they are doing something worthwhile for the kingdom of God. But once you get past the tourist shops, beautiful beaches, and high-rise resort hotels, life in the islands is gritty and poor and harsh.

As we came to see, family life in the Caribbean was in shambles. "Visiting marriages" were the norm. This is when men make a circuit of several women by whom they have several children, staying long enough to beget another before they become restless and move on. I saw the pressure toward immorality on the kids who were trying to serve the Lord in the midst of a culture that failed to define godly boundaries. Prejudice, racial violence, and crime were widespread, as were drug traffic and addiction, corrupt government officials, a variety of voodoo beliefs and juju men or witch doctors, grinding poverty, and the bizarre mixture of flesh and spirit. I actually saw a bar in Jamaica with the words "Watch and pray, for the Son of Man is coming at such a time as ye think not" painted above its door.

Yet none of this was visible as the cruise ships docked, disgorging flocks of tourists looking for the best souvenir bargains and clapping for the grinning entertainers who played traditional music on steel drums. The tourists didn't see what I saw: the grins were only part of the show.

playing peek-a-boo. When he hides his eyes, he thinks that you can't see him because he can't see you. Or do you remember, as a little kid, putting your hands over your ears and humming loudly when you didn't want to hear something? Are we like this when it comes to a suffering and lost world? Do we ever stop to think that the time we invest in reaching others for Christ carries *eternal* significance for them?

Campaigner for women in need, ministering life and kindness to females suffering cruel gender injustices. Preferably someone who can show forgiveness, understanding, and truth through cultural differences.

In every country, subculture, and socioeconomic background, women face injustice. These injustices range from small-scale inequalities, such as pressures to project a perfect image, to large-scale horrors, such as government-permitted abuse and sexual disfiguration. God has deep love for women and deep hatred for the crimes committed against them. Women are created in His image! His heart breaks for widows and unloved wives, and He takes seriously the treatment of children. As Christians, we are called to stand up against these tragedies.

- In developing countries, almost 50 percent of women between the ages of fifteen and forty-nine believe it is justifiable for husbands to beat their wives.
- Over 64 million women ages twenty to twenty-four report being married as children or teenagers.
- In Africa and Yemen, over 70 million girls have suffered sexual mutilation.
- Two-fifths of baby girls are aborted because of cultural preferences for sons.
- Two-thirds of the world's illiterate population are women.

Many of these statistics are interlinked. For example, people in some developing nations believe that early marriage protects a girl from poverty and abduction. However, child brides perpetuate gender inequality, as young girls are usually married to grown men, providing an immediate power dynamic that hurts the girl. Furthermore, these girls might become pregnant very early, and their little bodies have difficulty supporting the growing baby inside of them. These girls either die during the pregnancy or become child mothers. Young motherhood prohibits them from attending school, and so the gendered cycle of poverty is perpetuated. These circumstances can be factors in women joining the sex trade, forsaking education, and staying in abusive relationships. Christians must be the hands and feet of Jesus, committed to seeing healing and restoration brought to women in total brokenness.

In high school, Amy Giallanza took mission trips to five nations with King's Kids El Paso and felt God's call into full-time ministry. After some YWAM training, she moved to Australia to attend the Foundations of Counseling Ministry school. Through this school, Amy grew as a counselor but also grew in compassion and love for women. Her heart bled for girls who were never ascribed value or importance by their societies, and she desired to communicate worth and wholeness through Jesus. Amy set out to offer the most valuable resource she had: her time. She built relationships with women in detention centers, brothels, and crisis pregnancy centers. Alongside one-on-one counseling sessions about trust and hope, she started seminars on beauty, destiny, and identity. At twenty-seven years old, Amy has become the head of the Foundations of Counseling Ministry school in Perth and has ministered in eighteen countries. She continues to invest time, hope, and love into women all over the world.

It's your world—do something today!

Sponsor a young girl through Daughters of Cambodia. This Christian organization teaches practical trades and shares the gospel with women who would otherwise be caught in prostitution. Go to *www.daughtersofcambodia.org* for more information.

Be a voice for women and girls around you. Make the active decision to affirm and encourage girls in your school, church, and neighborhood. Stand up for those who are bullied by speaking truth and value into lives.

Proverbs 24:11–12

_____

_____

The second reason people object to mission work is that they haven't seen it for themselves. There are two very different categories of people who travel far from home and experience life in other nations: tourists and missionaries. Both tourists and missionaries take a lot of photos on their trips. Some of the most important pictures may not be the ones on camera. All Christians should have some pictures recorded on their hearts and minds to help keep their priorities straight. Mission outreaches provide lots of opportunities for God to show us new things, and not all the pictures will be happy ones.

Lamentations 3:51

_____

_____

When we see things that shake us up, the easiest response is denial. It must not be real. It must not be that bad. Somebody will do something about it. It hurts to let the full impact of other people's sufferings hit us. That can easily progress to excuses. It's not my job. I'm too busy. It's dangerous. It's too expensive to help.

But when we see something, we become responsible. Before, we could plead ignorance. Now there's no excuse not to do something. Seeing, really seeing, is costly. It can cost you the high-income career you had planned if God calls you to a different course. It can cost you all the self-indulgent living our TV commercials say is essential to happiness. It can cause you to lose interest in lower priorities.

Matthew 9:36

_____

_____

Are you willing to see—not just on the evening news on TV, which shows strangers far away who are suffering because of wars or disasters, but live and in person? It's easier not to see, but then we'll never have God's heart.

1 John 3:16–18

_____

_____

The Lord has a way of turning our heads toward a need at just the right time, of causing a door to open just as we walk by, of bringing an extraordinary opportunity. This is the exact opposite of our flesh, which tries hard to avoid anything unpleasant. Will you ask God to let you see? *Really* see? Will you ask Him not to spare you anything, but show you what is going on in the world around you? Then fasten your seat belt—you're in for some real spiritual growth!

REAL RELIGION

Real religion can't pass by a need and look the other way. It cares about people in trouble.

Matthew 25:40

_____

_____

James 1:27

_____

_____

God has a special interest in those the world ignores or exploits. All through Scripture He talks about the needs of widows, orphans, the fatherless, and foreigners. He sees what the lost could be like with their lives restored through a genuine relationship with Jesus. He sees a future full of hope for the poor and illiterate if they will come to Him. He has provision for all the widow's needs and strength for all the weak. God has a destiny planned for that grubby, runny-nosed little child.

1 Corinthians 1:26–29

_____

_____

1 Samuel 16:7

_____

_____

WRAP-UP

Let's wrap this up and apply it to our own lives. Let's put the teachings into a fresh prayer that sums up all we have seen this week.

Father, there are things I would rather not see or know about. But You see them, Lord, and I know they break Your heart. Help me to see more than I've seen before. Please give me a heart to make the personal sacrifices that You expect from me. I ask You to give me the courage and the compassion to never be an ostrich again. I don't want to live in a little bubble of self-centeredness. Help me to have goals for my life that are far higher than personal peace and affluence. Use my life to bring Your comfort to the hurting ones who have no comforter. Lord, show me my part in Your plan and how to take the right steps to get there. In Jesus' name. Amen.

What stands out to you in this prayer?

_____

_____

How will you put it into practice?

_____

_____

True Story

During a two-month outreach in India, we were exposed for the first time to the way much of the world lives. For sixteen years before that, we had led short missions outreaches to many countries, but this was a new experience altogether. Our family, with four children, slept on a stone floor on Indian-style mats. We bathed under a hose faucet and used the squatty potties. If you don't know about them, just use your imagination! Rats, mice, shrews, mosquitoes, flies, centipedes, and lizards came into our rooms and crawled on us while we slept. I knew I was getting used to being in India when I would wake up to something crawling on me, swat it, and not feel a need to turn on the flashlight to see what it was!

Each day we ate lots of rice, sitting on the floor in a building with no furniture, with two hundred flies buzzing around us. I learned to wave one hand over my plate while eating with the other, but the flies had already been on our food in the kitchen, which had no sink, refrigerator, or counters. Food was prepared on a newspaper or the bare floor and cooked on a camp stove. Every day we would squash up to fourteen people in a non-air-conditioned Indian SUV (with two people on the luggage rack on the roof) and drive for hours in the humid countryside to remote villages where the people had never seen a white person or heard of Jesus.

All of my sense of adventure and tourism ran out fast. This wasn't fun. Early on I realized that our American money and standards of comfort had been insulating us from the hard realities of life on all our previous outreaches. We could afford to put our teams in decent lodging, so we did. We could afford better food than the local people, so that's what we ate. And our transportation and bathroom facilities were better, all thanks to money. In America we don't know about much of the world's suffering. We're insulated from it.

If you plug in and pick up an extension cord, 110 (or 220) volts of electricity are flowing inside it. That's enough to stop your heart and kill you. Why don't you get hurt? Because the insulation protects you. On an outreach, things may be rougher than we are used to at home. Some of the insulation of life in America will be missing. Tourists won't stick it out, because their motive is pleasure. Missionaries don't think, *What's in this for me?* They come to serve, and they stay.

Tourists spend their time doing whatever is the most fun. Missionaries spend their time doing whatever will bless others and advance the kingdom of God. Tourists look at poverty and suffering from the air-conditioned comfort of a tour bus. Missionaries get busy doing something about it. Sure, we take time to enjoy the scenery, culture, and local food if possible. But what if God calls you to a place where the scenery and culture are dull and the food is awful? Tourists would stay home. Missionaries go for the glory of God and out of love for the people.

2 Timothy 2:3

_____

_____

_____

_____

Despite the hardships in India, we stuck it out. There were times we all wanted to go home, but God had sent us and we had a job to do. We've been back twice and are making plans for the next trip!

What has God been saying to you this week?

_____

_____

How does this affect your daily life?

_____

_____

How does this affect your life plans?

_____

_____

DAILY BIBLE READING

SCRIPTURE MEMORY

Galatians 5:13
Through love serve one another.

1 John 3:18 (NLT)
Dear children, let us stop just saying we love each other; let us really show it by our actions.

✔ Check when completed	
Sunday	Hosea 7–8
Monday	Hosea 9–11
Tuesday	Hosea 12–14
Wednesday	Joel 1–3
Thursday	Amos 1–2
Friday	Amos 3–5
Saturday	Amos 6–7

BIBLE READING QUESTIONS/THOUGHTS

_____
_____
_____
_____
_____
_____
_____
_____
_____
_____

PRAYER NEEDS THIS WEEK

_____
_____
_____
_____
_____
_____
_____

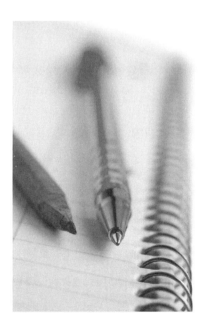

10

Lesson ten

THE CALLING TO SERVE

Most people have a very narrow definition of the word *serve* these days. Usually we hear it used in relation to food or sports. Restaurant staff serve our meals, and we take turns serving in volleyball, tennis, and Ping-Pong.

Galatians 5:13

_____

_____

Jesus had other ideas about serving. He said it was the characteristic of the highest-ranking people in God's kingdom. He told us even He was a servant and commanded us to serve others. If serving is that important, we should know more about it.

The right motivation for serving people is the one Jesus had in this story. He loved them and wanted to show it through practical means. It's one thing to say we love someone and another thing to show it consistently. In fact, people don't believe the words "I love you" if those words are not backed up by actions.

1 John 3:18 (read the New Living Translation quoted at the beginning of this lesson)

_____

_____

We don't need mushy feelings to serve others. Love is so much more than warm, fuzzy emotions, attraction, passion, or any other way we see it portrayed on TV or in books and movies. Love is wanting the greatest good for the other person. It's looking at others from God's perspective and valuing them as He does. In this way, we can love and serve strangers without knowing them personally, or even love a whole nation or another culture. When the Lord enables us to love others with His love, He will often call us to reach out and serve them.

Throughout your life as a Christian, you'll have the opportunity to love and serve people who are homeless, poor, younger and older than you, who speak another language, and who are very different from you. How can you love and serve them without really knowing them, or with just the beginning of a friendship and the knowledge that you probably won't see them again after you leave? Ask the Lord to give you His heart of compassion and love for them, and He will do it.

LAYING IT ASIDE

John 13:3–4 says, "Jesus, knowing that the Father had given all things into His hands, and that He had come from God and was going to God, rose from supper and laid aside His garments, took a towel and girded Himself." The key part of this story we'll look at in this lesson is that Jesus laid aside His garments. In other words, His robe would have gotten in the way of washing the disciples' feet, so He took it off and put it off to the side. In the same way, if you and I are going to be servants, we will also have to put aside things that would get in the way. The most important one of these things to lay aside is our pride.

Pride comes naturally. No one has to teach a little child to boast, and the older he or she grows, the more things there will be to boast about. Do you ever smile when you hear kids talk about themselves? Picture the nine-year-old boy telling his friends how he made the impossible shot in basketball, did the best skateboard stunt in history, or pulled off some other death-defying deed. The exaggeration is obvious to everyone but him. He's claiming a place of value and wants his friends to recognize it.

We constantly compare ourselves to others and keep score in our minds, until the Lord works in our hearts to teach us humility. Laying aside our pride means giving someone else that place of value. This comes easily to Christians who know their value comes not from our human accomplishments but from God, who loves us so much that He gave His Son for us. We no longer have to prove our worth

True Story

Kristin already told one story about the garbage dump in the Help Wanted section on page 100. Here's another story from the same location. It was our fourth outreach in the central Philippines. Delicate aromas wafted in to greet us when the van doors opened to the dump. The number of flies in one area was like the plague in Egypt. I kept processing these jolting experiences with the team and telling them God was resetting their poverty meter—the understanding of just how poor the poor can get.

A small child who lives there said, "We are the outcasts. Nobody loves us or cares about us. Thank you so much for loving us," reflecting the thoughts of many. All of us were struck as we went to Inayawan for the second summer and used our usual format of ministry, which has worked all over the world in a Third World setting. The sight of foreigners in matching shirts invading a neighborhood brings out mobs of curious children, so we stop at the local basketball court, field, or parking lot and start to play games with them. The delight on their faces shows through the language barrier. Then their parents come out to make sure the kids are safe and to satisfy their own curiosity. When a crowd of 200 to 400 forms, the local pastors introduce us and we begin a gospel presentation, followed by prayer for people to meet the Lord, physical healing for the sick, and help for a multitude of needs. At the end, it's back to playing with the kids. When we leave, we're glad we had the opportunity to love these people. We care about them, just as God does.

But this time we heard about a way to put our faith and message into action. The Philippine government had offered a way out of living in shacks on top of the trash to some of the families. There was land available and the promise of affordable loans if the people would put their own labor into building homes. The question came to us—would the American team help them? It would mean clearing brush, leveling land, carrying cinder blocks and water, and mixing cement in the oppressive heat and humidity of the jungle.

We jumped in! It was a full two days of serious labor, while for some strange reason the local government building played John Philip Sousa music at ear-shattering levels. It was bugs and lizards, laughing and getting filthy, working alongside the poorest of the poor, with a language barrier that kept us from understanding each other but not from making friends. It was exhausting and satisfying, with deep appreciation from the families who could soon move their children away from the disease and dangers of the dump. It was worth it.

to ourselves or others. There's a place of security and confidence that only Christians can know, and this is the basis for laying aside our pride to serve others.

Next, we must lay aside laziness. Some people recognize that this is a strong tendency in their lives, but all of us can be lazy sometimes. It's easy to make excuses not to do things we know we should do. Laziness is sitting in the shade until someone else gets up first when there's work to be done. It's being the last one to move toward the task. It's not volunteering and hoping someone else will. It's

Relief worker to serve in areas of natural disasters and emergencies. Must be determined to cling to Jesus' hope and mercy in wretched conditions.

The frequency of natural disasters is increasing. Statistics from the World Bank and the Natural Disasters Data Book show the following:

- In 1970 fewer than 100 natural disasters were reported, but in 2005 there were more than 400 disasters.
- In 2011 natural disasters around the world killed 28,800 people and affected over 85 million people.
- The 2011 disasters caused financial damage of nearly $290 billion.

Tsunamis, fires, earthquakes, and hurricanes devastate lives, causing people to feel utterly hopeless. In developing nations, this devastation is compounded, as there is often little help from government agencies.

For a few minutes, imagine that a tsunami destroyed everything you own, including the crops and livestock your family uses as income. You have no food, no house, no clothes, and no way to make money. You panic because you can't find a job due to the thousands of other people who are looking for work, and the flooding in the streets has posed serious health threats: mosquitoes that carry fatal diseases, a broken sewage system, overloaded hospitals and total strangers living in close quarters. In this situation, what would you do? Where would you sleep? What if you couldn't find food, clean water, or medical attention? Where would you go for help?

Every year, thousands of people around the world find themselves in this type of hopeless situation. The body of Christ has a responsibility to help, yet many people just watch the news and then just continue their daily lives. When whole cities and countries have experienced a horrible tragedy, Christians must rise up and demonstrate hope! We can love our neighbors practically by donating money, clothes, canned food, medical supplies, and time to people who literally have nothing else. By sharing material things alongside the gospel of Jesus, we can provide tremendous relief to a person or family who otherwise has nothing. The next time you hear about a natural disaster, make the decision to provide aid for people who are in urgent need of help.

In 2011 wildfires raged throughout areas surrounding Austin, Texas, destroying over one thousand homes. In response to this disaster, the seventh-grade class of a Christian school named Veritas Academy asked the school districts to provide a list of all other seventh graders who had lost their homes. Each seventh-grade student from Veritas adopted another student who had been affected by the fires and provided major items that the family had lost. One Veritas student was even able to get a piano donated for a student who had lost his piano to the fires! Through this experience, Veritas Academy showed Christlike love to many families in their area, demonstrating the hope of Jesus to people in a very difficult situation.

It's your world—do something today!

Ask your school, church, or family to reserve a closet specifically for victims of natural disasters. Through the year, fill this closet with unwanted clothes, toys, canned goods, and medical supplies. The next time you hear of a natural disaster, you will already have boxes of vital items ready to ship out.

Looking for more training or a long-term place of service to disaster victims? YWAM has a three-month training school called the School of Emergency Services and Disaster Response in San Diego, California. Look it up at *http://ywamsandiegobaja.org*.

halfheartedly helping but knowing that you're only putting out the minimum effort so you'll look like you're involved and not get in trouble. We are experts in disguising our selfishness.

Another thing to lay aside is busyness. We are constantly on the go. There's always more to do than we have time to get done. Even when we feel bored, it's not that there's nothing to do; it's that there's nothing we really *want* to do. The big question is our priorities. We can always find time to do the things that benefit ourselves, but it takes effort to carve out time from a busy schedule to do the things that benefit others—especially if we know there will probably be no thanks, reward, or recognition.

The best judges of our servanthood are the people who live with us. They know what we're really like. If you want to know how much of a servant you are, ask your mother or roommate or spouse. They can see how much self-sacrifice or selfishness is in your life. God's call to servanthood will have a different application for each of us. He calls each of us to some form of laying down our life for others. What do you need to lay aside to be a servant?

A Dirty Job

The story continues: "After that, He poured water into a basin and began to wash the disciples' feet, and to wipe them with the towel with which He was girded" (John 13:5). What was it like for Jesus to wash the disciples' feet? Although it's impossible for us to say how He felt at that moment, we can look at Scripture and think through Jesus' incredible action.

Philippians 2:3–8

_____

_____

Have you ever been in a place that was so dirty and gross that you just wanted to get out before you caught something? How about a place with revolting smells that made you gag, or vapor that made your eyes burn, or lots of bugs or rats or other unwelcome critters? We've been in lots of places like this on mission trips to slums around the world. Yet some people live under those conditions, and it never bothers them—because they are used to it. The reason these settings bother us so much is that they are so very different from what we are accustomed to.

In the same way, the gap between what heaven is like and what earth is like is enormous. We think earth is beautiful, and it still does demonstrate God's glory, but the whole galaxy is fallen and corrupt because of sin. The best of what creation has to offer isn't on the same scale as the perfection of God's dwelling place in heaven. For God, even looking at the earth that is so far below Him is humbling.

Psalm 113:4–6

_____

_____

It's not just a question of *distance,* as in light years or miles. Jesus came to earth despite the unimaginable *difference* between heaven and earth. And He didn't come with an oxygen mask and rubber gloves. No biohazard suit or disinfectants. He fully experienced life as a man. To top it off, Jesus didn't come to live in luxury in the finest palace of the richest king, eating the best food and wearing the most excellent clothes, as if that would have made any difference in earth being more like His home in heaven. He lived the way an ordinary person would every day for thirty-three years, and on this particular night in Jerusalem He voluntarily took on the job reserved for the lowest slave. He washed the dirty feet of men who would soon betray Him and even deny knowing Him, and Jesus knew in advance this would happen.

Why would He do it? Because He loved them that much and wanted to show them a pattern to follow. Can you picture Him holding His breath and trying to get it done as quickly as possible, with a look of distaste on His face? No way! Jesus the Lord was also Jesus the servant, and His actions came from a heart full of love for humans as sinful, selfish, and fallen as you and I are. He did it willingly and gladly. If we ask Him, He can teach us to serve others that way.

Not My Feet!

"Peter said to Him, 'You shall never wash my feet!'" (John 13:8). Why would Peter have such a strong reaction? After all, Jesus had made it clear that He was going to wash their feet. Who was Peter to challenge the Lord?

Maybe Peter was thinking back to the time he saw Jesus transfigured: suddenly Jesus hadn't looked like the carpenter's son but like He does in heaven now.

Matthew 17:2

_____

_____

Peter might have been remembering hearing a voice like thunder as God the Father spoke to them.

Matthew 17:5

_____

_____

He would surely never forget his response to being in the presence of his Creator.

Matthew 17:6

_____

_____

It could be that Peter was thinking of Jesus' awesome displays of divine power and authority in healing cripples, casting out demons, calming the storm, or multiplying loaves and fishes. Whatever memories came to Peter's mind at that time, he clearly felt uneasy at the thought of the Lord Jesus Christ stooping to wash the mud and dung off his feet. It was unthinkable! The roles should have been reversed. Peter ought to have had the towel and basin to wash his Master's feet.

But Jesus explained a little more, and Peter finally understood that having Jesus wash his feet was symbolic of being washed from his sins, so he stopped arguing. The attitude of Peter's heart is the point we need to look at here. Peter realized his place (a simple fisherman, an ordinary man, a sinner) in relation to Jesus' place as Lord and God. All his previous boastful, self-filled, swaggering, macho attitudes grew silent. He must have felt humble awe as Jesus took the towel in His hand, the Creator serving the creation.

An Example

"For I have given you an example, that you should do as I have done to you" (John 13:15). Do you think that Jesus meant that we should literally wash the feet of others, or is this symbolic? Maybe both! If you've ever participated in a foot-washing ceremony at a church or youth camp, you probably remember that there were tears as people humbled themselves, asked forgiveness, and showed how much they valued each other. The times that people have washed my feet in Mexico, India, and China were powerful memories of our relationships with good friends there.

Back in Bible days, the need for washing dirty feet was obvious. People wore sandals and walked wherever they went. Muddy roads and all the souvenirs left behind as camels, horses, donkeys, cows, and sheep walked on those roads made for a pretty gross journey. When they arrived at their destinations, getting clean was a priority, and washing the feet of guests was a way to make them feel special (Luke 7:44; 1 Timothy 5:10).

Some places are still like this. I've walked to villages that couldn't be reached by SUV after the Indian summer monsoons. The mud and special ingredients sucked the sandals off our feet and squooshed up through our toes and over our ankles. Our youngest was small enough for a piggyback ride through the blocks of mire, but the rest of us badly needed the foot washing offered by the lone Christian family in the village.

During a conference for a hundred-plus rural pastors in India, the leader asked if both American men would wash the pastors' feet. This was easy for us to do, since we went as servants. The heavily calloused feet of these farmer/pastors, with the mud and whatever else was on them, quickly turned the water brown. The washing was an important means of communicating our equality and respect for them, showing that we didn't think we were better

True Story

A church in downtown Asunción, Paraguay, opens up every Saturday morning for homeless children to come for a hot meal. Our team arrived to a chaotic scene that scared many of them.

About fifty kids who live by begging or stealing showed up that day. Most of their mothers are prostitutes, and the girls join the profession at age twelve. If they have fathers at home, they are usually addicts or alcoholics. Sniffing shoe polish is the most common high. Our kids were in shock over the children's condition and behavior—violent and virtually uncontrollable. Ranging from two to twelve years old, the children were barefoot and wearing layers of ragged clothes to keep warm on a bitter cold winter's morning. They were a heart-wrenching sight.

We were there to serve a meal and present the gospel message. The pastor told us that when they first started ministering to the children, as soon as the food was brought out, the children would erupt in violence to be sure they got some. It took the leaders a long time to teach them to sit in their chairs and not brawl to get to the front of the line. The children had to learn to trust the leaders to provide enough, and to overcome the feral tendency to fight to get their food. They sat in rows of chairs and tables, violence simmering under the surface as the meal simmered in the kitchen.

After a simple meal of rice with flecks of chicken, yuca root (a starch we ate regularly there), and bananas, we watched as one boy scraped everyone's leftovers off their plates into a bag and took it home. That sounds revolting to us, but for them it was just part of survival. We took an offering and collected over two hundred dollars from the team to buy food for the church to feed the kids.

than them because we were more educated, wealthier foreigners. We honored them as our brothers in Christ.

However, now that literal foot washing is more symbolic than necessary in most of our lives, we should see if there are other ways to fulfill the principles that foot washing shows. How can you make people you value highly know how you feel? If you have strained relationships with others, what would be the best way to humble yourself and make things right? Are there people in your life who are beaten down and feel worthless? Can you communicate how precious they are to the Lord by your words and actions?

Just Do It!

"If you know these things, blessed are you if you do them" (John 13:17).

We all know a lot more than we actually live out. It's like the old saying, "When all is said and done, there's a lot more said than done."

Humans are very skilled at thinking up excuses not to do what we should do. (We also find ways to justify doing things that we shouldn't do, but that's another message entirely.) Picture a few common situations with me:

Your mom says she's really tired, and you know she's coming down with a cold. As she sighs and looks at the big pile of dishes in the sink, you know what she's thinking, so you . . .

1. look extra busy with your homework.
2. turn back to the major text drama taking place on your cell phone. After all, Ruben just broke up with Laura because he's going after Lisa, but what he doesn't know is that she thinks he's a real loser and is totally into William, who . . .
3. wait for her to ask you to do the dishes, then sigh back at her real loud and stomp over to the sink.
4. ask her to sit down and say you'll make her some tea and then clean the kitchen.

Your neighbor's yard looks like a jungle. In fact, strange animal noises come from there. The elderly couple who live there have had a lot of health problems lately, so you . . .

1. hope they get a ticket from the police for having such an ugly yard.
2. call the police to make sure they get the ticket.
3. go next door and offer to do their yard for $50.
4. call a couple of your friends and give up a Saturday together to help them.

You know God has called you into the ministry. You have studied the Bible and prepared the greatest message since the Sermon on the Mount. You approach the pastor and tell him you would like a Sunday service to preach this great revelation. He smiles kindly and says he doesn't think that will work right now but that the church really does need help with setting up chairs and painting the bathrooms, so you . . .

1. stomp out and change churches immediately.
2. tell him you're really too busy for that and start looking for a place that will appreciate your many gifts and talents.

3. tell all your friends how sad it is that the pastor is so out of touch with God.

4. ask him where the paint rollers are and when to come set up the chairs.

Now score your answers. Give yourself one million points for every #4 and subtract one million points for every other answer. How do you think Jesus rates your servanthood?

Wrap-up

Let's wrap this up and put it into a fresh prayer that reflects what we're learning about serving others.

Father, I'm a lot better at being served than I am at serving. It's hard for me to lay aside my pride, laziness, and busyness, but I want to become a servant and I need Your help. Will You work in my heart so I'll want to show love to others in practical ways, even when it costs my time and energy? Will You help me learn to make sacrifices instead of being selfish so I can show Your love to others? Will You transform my life so that it shows people around me what You are like? In Jesus' name. Amen.

What stands out to you in this prayer?

_____

_____

How will you put it into practice?

_____

_____

What has God been saying to you this week?

_____

_____

How does this affect your daily life?

_____

_____

How does this affect your life plans?

_____

_____

SCRIPTURE MEMORY

1 John 2:17
And the world is passing away, and the lust of it; but he who does the will of God abides forever.

Matthew 6:33
But seek first the kingdom of God and His righteousness, and all these things shall be added to you.

DAILY BIBLE READING

✓ Check when completed	
Sunday	Amos 8–9
Monday	Obadiah
Tuesday	Jonah 1–2
Wednesday	Jonah 3–4
Thursday	Micah 1–2
Friday	Micah 3–5
Saturday	Micah 6–7

BIBLE READING QUESTIONS/THOUGHTS

_____
_____
_____
_____
_____
_____
_____
_____
_____
_____

PRAYER NEEDS THIS WEEK

_____
_____
_____
_____
_____
_____
_____
_____
_____

11

RECEIVING A KINGDOM

Did you go to the beach as a child? Along with the smell of suntan lotion, finding seashells, and playing in the water, your memories probably include building sand castles. The wet sand was the perfect medium for expressing your architectural abilities. Maybe you put lots of effort into building a magnificent castle, only to find that when the tide came in, it was swept away. There's no way to hold back the tide! No matter how elaborate your castle was, all that's left of it now are memories and photos. Sand castles just don't last.

I researched sand castles and found out there are international sand-castle competitions each year. (There are even international rock-paper-scissors competitions.) The winning sand castles are amazing. On my best day with my plastic pail and shovel, I could never come close to these creations.

There are not only sand-castle competitions but also ice-sculpture competitions with displays that are incredible. Yet if we all got on a plane to go see last year's winning ice sculpture in person, sadly it wouldn't be there anymore, just like the winning sand castles.

Once, when our family was praying at home, our eldest daughter had an impression: The opposite of God's kingdom is a sand castle. Hebrews 12:28–29 says, "Since we are receiving a kingdom which cannot be shaken, let us have grace, by which we may serve God acceptably with reverence and godly fear. For our God is a consuming fire." Unlike the temporary nature of sand castles and ice sculptures, God's kingdom is lasting.

TWO KINGDOMS

During our seventy or so years that God gives us on earth, we will all put lots of effort and energy into building something—a reputation or legacy of some sort. The question is, will it last? What will we build it out of, and where will we build it?

A life set on building an earthly kingdom out of earthly materials can achieve impressive results. People may marvel at our accomplishments, envy our status, or covet our possessions. We may receive acclaim as the best sand-castle builders around. Great sand-castle builders write books about how they made it to the top, and those who want to follow in their footsteps eagerly read them. They forget it's all temporary. It's shakable and impermanent and cannot last.

God's Word tells us everything that is shakable will be shaken (Hebrews 12:27). We live in shaky times right now, with economic troubles, an increase in terror, wars and rumors of war, plagues, governments toppling, hurricanes and tornadoes, floods and tsunamis, and earthquakes in many places. Does this sound a little like Scripture to you?

But God promises something sure, something to hold on to. I was in L.A. just after the devastating Northridge earthquake in 1994. Around 4:00 a.m. a strong aftershock hit, and I held on to my bed, wondering whether this was the "big one." When the earth shakes, people want to grab on to something solid. When people's lives shake, they need to grab on to the Lord. His kingdom isn't made of sand! Let's contrast the two kingdoms.

Earthly Kingdom	Kingdom of Heaven
Temporary	Eternal
Visible	Invisible

In addition to being temporary, the earthly kingdom is loud. The best example of this is ads on TV. They turn up the volume so we can still hear the commercials when we run to the refrigerator. The earthly kingdom is also dazzling and attention grabbing. If you've ever walked through Times Square in New York or along the Strip in Las Vegas, you know the sensory assault of flashing, brightly colored lights and videos and noises vying for your attention.

The loud and the temporary come at us from all sides, claiming the right to be the focus of our attention. So much is going on 24/7, with so many demands on our time and thoughts. We're told to achieve so many goals and told we need so many things that the invisible kingdom of God gets pushed to the back burner of our lives.

LIVING IN A TEMPORARY WORLD

We need temporary things to live in the temporary world. Most of these things are fine, in their place, which is out on the fringes of our lives. The problem for us is when a distraction becomes a focus, when a temporary thing parks itself directly before us. It's so hard to keep our priorities straight. Both the problems and pleasures of this life crowd in tightly around us and clamor for our attention. We become absorbed by the cares of this life and forget there's anything more. We forget we're creatures made for a different world, and we lose ourselves in this one.

Psalm 16:8

_____

_____

Matthew 6:33

_____

_____

What's the center of your life? What's your focus? Has something temporary consumed your attention?

- A relationship that we thought would last? How many of us have found out that relationships are shakable?
- Achieving success? Ask any former rock star, athlete, or has-been actor about success.
- A career? Uncertain economic times, corporate downsizing, and the failure of even large companies make this area of life uncertain.

- Riches? Stock markets crash, investments prove unreliable, and inflation takes away the value of savings.
- Beauty? Notice how frequently Hollywood throws away the leading actors and actresses in favor of new ones who are younger and better looking.

If a shakable thing is your focus, remember that the only thing that cannot be shaken is God's kingdom. The question is whether or not you are receiving it and allowing the Lord to wean you from the temporary.

True Story

My wife and I were newly married and just starting out in ministry. By day we taught in a Christian school, and I was also the youth pastor in a growing church, which kept us busy many nights. The pay was ridiculously little, but the satisfaction was immense. As we furnished our tiny apartment and then our starter home, one of the things I really wanted was a good stereo. We didn't have or want a TV, but Christian music was important to us.

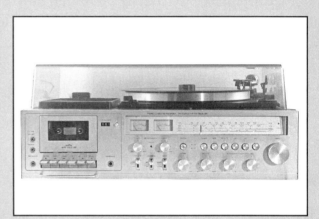

As I studied the specs on speakers, equalizers, amplifiers, and—don't laugh—cassette players and turntables, a dilemma presented itself. God was working powerfully in my life. I spent many hours in prayer, nose in the carpet, and hours studying my Bible. The call to die to self and a burden for this lost world was growing stronger with me each day. Eternity was becoming real, and the sense of responsibility to make a difference in the world was consuming me. I wanted to see people come to Jesus and wept for the lost teenagers of our city. How could something as trivial and mundane as having a nice stereo also interest me? I felt worldly and carnal, but I still wanted one.

Slowly an understanding of the place of things in the Christian life became clear. God doesn't call us to asceticism—living a stark and plain life as a matter of principle. He gives us all things to enjoy (1 Timothy 6:17), yet we do have a responsibility to bridle our appetites for selfish fulfillment. Scripture doesn't define specific details for us about how much is too much.

Should we have six pairs of shoes? How about sixty? Remembering that many people have no shoes at all can curb our greed. Should a Christian live in a two-thousand-square-foot house? What about a ten-thousand-square-foot house? How lavishly should it be furnished? Having a good car is necessary for many of us in our culture. But what about a convertible sports car to drive just on the weekends and a couple of dirt bikes and a quad and a boat and jet skis? How full should a closet be, and do we as believers keep up with fashion trends designed to keep money flowing from our pockets into those of the clothing designers? Cutting-edge electronics, the latest gaming systems, vacations . . . what captures your thoughts? If the money is available or can be borrowed, wants can become needs in our minds. There's no end to our lust for things. The eyes of man are *never* satisfied (Proverbs 27:20). Where should Christians draw the line?

At last I settled on a balance. I pledged to the Lord, on our very limited salary, to give as much money to missions as I spent on each part of my dream stereo setup. This was a big step of faith for me, and I thought it would probably take forever to complete my plan. But God surprised me as I came across the most incredible sales on the exact components I wanted. I fulfilled my promise to send an equal sum to advance God's kingdom overseas. I felt joy in giving and enjoyment in listening to my new stereo.

Eventually my stereo became old, and various parts broke down. They all went into garage sales for mission outreaches. Things perish with the using (Colossians 2:22), but the results of the equal amount of money I gave to the Lord will last forever.

Ultimately, we have to decide what is more real—the things we can feel and see around us or the invisible realm of God. We'll have to settle on whether we believe God's Word is true or not and whether or not we believe in eternity. Then we will weigh our seventy years against forever and live accordingly. We'll see the foolishness of people whose visions don't go past their own funerals.

It's like remodeling your home in Jericho when Joshua and the Israelites are marching around it for the last time.

It's like putting the finishing touches on a new house while Noah hammers away at the ark next door.

Psalm 17:14

_____

_____

Think about where you're building your life. Remember the great sand castle you once built where the high tide could flood it. High tides are inevitable. So is God's judgment of this world and all that's in it. When our daily focus is on the things of this world—fantasizing about them, acquiring them, collecting them, maintaining them, replacing them—we would have to say our life is here.

1 John 2:17

_____

_____

But we find ourselves jealous of those with bigger sand castles. So often, we are still in pursuit of the temporary.

Psalm 119:57

_____

_____

The contrast is found in people who can look ahead and realize that this world is temporary. There's no sense in building a sand castle when the tide is coming in. It's pointless to build a life with no lasting results.

People have one of two basic philosophies about life:

1. Try to get the most enjoyment out of the temporary things as they slip through our fingers like sand.
2. Receive an eternal kingdom.

1 Timothy 6:17

_____

_____

Anything that has to be received can also be rejected. It's not automatic. God gives, but we have to receive. I hope some people reading this chapter will receive a kingdom that can't be shaken. Faith helps us postpone the payoff. It gets us past the immaturity of thinking about what feels good right now and helps us see that every action has a consequence. Faith causes us to see that this world isn't our home. We realize that we were made for another place, and we stop trying to fit in here.

Philippians 3:18–20

_____

_____

Ecclesiastes 3:11

_____

_____

God designed you for eternity. That's why you can't find any lasting satisfaction in temporary things. There's a place in your life that only God can fill.

Living in the Light of Eternity

The light of eternity must shine in our hearts and minds, our attitudes and direction, our life goals, and our purposes for living even now. Through God's revelation to our hearts of eternal truth, He aims us away from materialism and toward love for others, away from selfishness and toward servanthood, away from squandering our time and toward investing it in things that will last: the will of God, pointing others to Christ, and living as examples of obedience and faith. We'll become better stewards of the resources and money that flow through our hands and seek to use everything at our disposal for God's glory.

Speaking of squandering our time, here's a challenge that will make you think. Many people think they are too busy to read the Bible, pray, or serve others, but all of us have twenty-four hours in each day. Is there something you spend a couple of hours on each day as you relax and unwind from a busy day at work or school? It may be two hours on your favorite video game, a movie, Facebook, the latest series on Netflix, or working out. But if you have a daily recreation or entertainment routine that takes two hours (or sometimes much more), then let's do a little math. At the end of the year, you will have put a solid month, day and night, into that thing. Was your time invested or wasted? What do you have to show for your use of two hours each day? Or if you're a four-hour-a-day video-game junkie, that's two solid months out of your year!

When you're eighty-five years old and the clock is ticking on your lifespan or the doctor says your days are limited, will you regret the time you squandered and can never get back?

> When I stand at the Judgment Seat of Christ
> And He shows His plan for me,
> The plan of my life as it might have been
> Had He had His way—and I see
> How I blocked Him here, and checked Him there,
> And I would not yield my will,

Will there be grief in my Savior's eyes,
Grief though He loves me still?
Would He have me rich and I stand there poor,
Stripped of all but His grace,
While memory runs like a hunted thing,
Down the paths I cannot retrace.
Lord, of the years that are left to me
I give them to Thy hand
Take me and break me and mold me,
To the pattern that Thou hast planned!
—Author unknown

Psalm 90:12

_____

_____

1 John 2:15–17

_____

_____

Hebrews 1:10–12

_____

_____

The Lord compares creation to an old garment. It was new once and looked really nice. Now it's old and used up—it's in pretty sorry shape. It wasn't meant to last forever. It has served its purpose, and soon it will be discarded. Imagine that God can take the entire universe in His hands, fold it up, and throw it away!

2 Peter 3:7, 10

_____

_____

There are two parts to the visible side of creation—what God made (the earth) and what men have made from it (the things that are in it). God made the avocados, but we make the guacamole. All of it will be burned up someday, along with all the things that people strive after, including power, fame, status, and popularity. There's only one exception—the eternal souls of men and women. People last forever, but nothing else will remain.

Creation itself will be remade into new heavens and a new earth (2 Peter 3:13; Revelation 21:1–2). Our weak and temporary human bodies will be exchanged for resurrected, eternal bodies that will never again get sick, grow old, or die (1 Corinthians 15:35–54).

So on one side we have things that are temporary and on the other side the only part of the visible universe that will last forever—people. Each day you and I trade our lives for one or the other. Other people, like employers or schoolteachers, may have a claim on much of our time, but we can always decide what to do with our lives.

The motivation behind why you live is always your decision. Stop for a minute to think about what you yearn and long for. Consider what thoughts fill your free moments and reflect your hopes and dreams and then categorize them as being part of the temporary world or as having eternal value.

True Story

Renee spent her teenage summers in Ethiopia, India, Russia, Mexico, and Indonesia. Her tender heart was the door into the lives of many people to whom we ministered on these outreaches. One day in Ethiopia, after we had ministered in the Mother Teresa home for handicapped children and to countless street people, she wrote this poem.

After college Renee became a teacher, but instead of applying at a normal school in the United States, she went to a Muslim nation in the Middle East, where it's illegal to share the gospel. Her goal is to befriend Muslim women, one of the hardest of all populations to reach because of their isolation in the strict societal structures, and indeed it has been frustrating. After a year, she told me she has yet to make a single Muslim friend. She's sticking it out and has renewed her contract to teach there, but I think most people would have given up by now.

When I saw her recently, I asked if it would be OK to tell our local Intensive Discipleship Course group of about twenty teenagers her story so they could pray for her. She said, "Oh yes! Please!" Maybe you can pray for Renee, too. Maybe you can follow her example and be a light in a dark place someday, too.

My Love for Today

Beautiful child
Big brown eyes
Dark face, braided hair
She leans on me and cries
I hold her close
To sing and pray
You're my baby girl
My love for today

Beautiful child
Crooked teeth
Cold clasping hands
I feel him breathe
Safe in my arms
I sing and pray
You're my baby boy
My love for today

Beautiful child
Precious and real
I ask our Father
To comfort and heal
Beautiful child
Alive and true
I see the face of Jesus in you

Beautiful woman
Tired and worn tears
Dirty clothes, aged face
God knows your fears
My mouth speaks truth
We sing and pray
You're my big sister
My love for today

Beautiful man
Strong handshake
You tell me your story
Both our hearts break
The connection is made
We sing and pray
You're my big brother
My love for today

Beautiful person
Precious and real
I plead with our Father
To comfort and heal
Beautiful person
Alive and true
I see the heart of Jesus in you.

A respected Bible teacher says that most people trade their days for dollars and their dollars for things and then they die. What a futile and meaningless pursuit! Jesus said that one's life does not consist in the abundance of the things one possesses (Luke 12:15). The greater reason for life is the purpose God created each of us to fulfill.

The best way I know to examine my own life and see whether my priorities and values are in line with God's will is to look at this life from the perspective of eternity. In a thousand years, what difference will it make if I ever lived? What difference will today make in a thousand years? Is the one life I'll ever have going to count?

The purpose God created us to fulfill is far greater than pursuing pleasure, satisfaction, and self-fulfillment.

Whether we see Jesus return in the clouds or whether a truck runs a red light and sends us into the presence of God tomorrow, we will all be caught by surprise and yanked from this temporary place into forever. Jesus said He would come when we don't expect it. Then God will ask us what we did with our lives.

Daniel 7:9–10

_____

_____

This brief passage puts things into perspective. For the man or woman standing before the throne of God, fame and power are now trivial and insignificant. All the things people yearn for and all the possessions they gave their lives to obtain are trifles.

Those who know Jesus have the assurance that their sins are forgiven, yet the Bible says we will all stand before the judgment seat of Christ and receive the reward for the things we did while we lived in our bodies. Picture it like this for the redeemed: when we get there, the Lord says, "You can come in and stay here forever, but first we'll look at what you did with the one life I gave you."

This may be a shock even for genuine Christians who didn't plan their lives with an eternal perspective. Consider a successful, born-again businessman who discovers that he has no results from his life that carry over into forever. Or a Christian Olympic athlete who shows off his five gold medals and God says, "Gold, eh? We make streets out of that stuff up here. Hand them to the angel—maybe we can melt them down and fill in a pothole. Now tell Me—what did you do with your life?"

There's nothing wrong with being a successful businessman or an Olympic athlete if people use the place God gives them in life for a higher reason than becoming rich or famous. But if they live for themselves, they'll have nothing eternal to show for it. God will look at the results of their lives, shake His head sadly, and say, "Put all the results of your life in the pile with that old coat. None of those things matter here."

Think back to when you were a child. Do you remember all the things you wanted for Christmas so badly when you were six or eight years old? Where are they now? Doesn't it seem silly that you absolutely couldn't live without a Barbie or a skateboard or something else?

1 Corinthians 13:11

_____

_____

Right-to-life advocate on behalf of millions of children who are murdered annually through abortion. Must have firm convictions on the value and importance of life. Must be willing to stand through controversy.

Every year, millions of preborn children are murdered through the violent destruction of their bodies. These children feel pain, fight to survive, and sometimes attempt to escape death within their mothers' wombs by fleeing from probes, suction devices, and metal tools. Heartbreakingly, legal abortion is permitted and even celebrated as evidence of human rights progress in most First World countries. The vocabulary, political arguments, and phrases used by leading voices in the media can make the topic of abortion confusing—even in Christian circles. This generation must choose to look at what God says about human life rather than what our news stations and government officials say about it. Furthermore, we must actively decide to be the voice of the preborn, persuading others to value their precious lives.

- Worldwide, there are an estimated 40 million abortions per year.
- Almost 25 percent of all pregnancies end in abortion.
- Two-fifths of all baby girls are aborted.
- Clinics in the United States perform 1.1 million abortions each year, which is the highest rate of all developed countries.
- *A baby's heart beats by the third week of pregnancy.*

Abortionists do not consider preborn babies to be humans, because of their location, size, function, and dependency on the mother. However, we consider the people around us to be human, regardless of their location, size, function, or dependency on others. As Christians, we know that God cares tremendously about all preborn children. He has knit each baby together in his or her mother's womb. The genocide toll of the preborn is greater than that of any other war, including the current wars in Africa and the millions killed in World War II. These invaluable lives are worth protecting with the same passion that we feel toward the humans around us. For more information on a Christian perspective of abortion, visit *www.bound4life.com*.

It's your world—do something today!

Be a courageous voice that frequently speaks on behalf of the preborn. Stand up for them in classes, debates, and casual conversation. Many people are not educated on the issue of abortion but take a pro-choice stance merely because they are swayed by celebrities and news sources. Be a firm voice that influences others toward a biblical love for the preborn. Additionally, join a group that actively promotes life. Look for Students for Life on your campus (*www.studentsforlife.org*), or begin a group.

Continue your pro-life activism even after a child is born. Volunteer with Christian adoption agencies, such as Generations Adoptions, which reach out to women in crisis pregnancy centers and then encourages them to place their child for adoption. Go to *www.generationsadoptions.org* to find out how to help, or volunteer at your local crisis pregnancy center.

Now those things don't seem so important. Think of any things you want right now—any life goals that aren't eternal, any things with a price tag—where will they be in ten years, much less a thousand? As the old hymn says, "Turn your eyes upon Jesus. Look full in His wonderful face, and the things of earth will grow strangely dim in the light of His glory and grace."

Colossians 3:2

Ephesians 4:15

_____

_____

Think of this world like a carnival. Carnivals are a lot of fun but they're just passing through town. They are a diversion from real life, not real life. We go there to be entertained, to forget about stresses and problems for a while. We get filled up on hot dogs and cotton candy, then play the games and ride the rides. If you win at a carnival game, what do you get? A kazoo, a plastic bracelet, or, if you really win big, maybe a stuffed teddy bear.

Mark 8:34–37

_____

_____

The carnival of this world is run by Satan. The Bible calls him the god of this world (2 Corinthians 4:4). He has tricked most people into playing silly games for worthless prizes. We're so captivated by the bright lights and music that we forget what's really important. What will happen when the Lord comes and snatches us by surprise out of the carnival and into heaven?

The greatest human achievements, the most sought-after possessions, will look about as valuable as a Happy Meal toy. How will we feel when misplaced priorities, selfish living, and lack of concern about the eternal souls of people catch up to us? And when the Lord says, "You missed it! I didn't send you into the carnival to win the prizes. I sent you there to win the people!"

This is a call to live for a higher reason: being part of God's plan to affect the course of people's destiny and change the course of history. Whether it's in your own country or in a foreign land, it's exciting to be able to say, "Lord, use me today to have an everlasting impact on someone. Let me do something today that will affect eternity."

WRAP-UP

Let's wrap this up and apply it to our own lives. This week we've contrasted the temporary and the eternal through numerous illustrations (the old coat, sand castles, ice sculptures, toys, and carnivals). Let's put it into a fresh prayer that sums up all we have seen this week.

Father, it would be so easy for me to live with my eyes and heart set on the temporary things it seems everyone else wants. Your Word tells me they are just part of the old coat that You will someday fold up and discard. Help me when the lust for possessions hits again. Show me how to get my priorities straight and keep them straight. Let me see clearly and not be deceived by the carnival. I don't want to waste the few years I have on earth playing silly games for worthless prizes. Help me see into forever! In Jesus' name. Amen.

What stands out to you in this prayer?

_____

_____

How will you put it into practice?

_____

_____

What has God been saying to you this week?

_____

_____

How does this affect your daily life?

_____

_____

How does this affect your life plans?

_____

_____

SCRIPTURE MEMORY

Proverbs 24:11–12
Deliver those who are drawn
    toward death,
And hold back those stum-
    bling to the slaughter.
If you say, "Surely we did not
    know this,"
Does not He who weighs the
    hearts consider it?
He who keeps your soul, does
    He not know it?
And will He not render to
    each man according to his
    deeds?

James 4:17
Therefore, to him who knows
to do good and does not do
it, to him it is sin.

FILL OUT SELF-
EVALUATION 2 ON THE
NEXT PAGE

FILL OUT THE COURSE
EVALUATION ON PAGE 158

DAILY BIBLE READING

✓ Check when completed	
Sunday	Nahum and Habakkuk
Monday	Zephaniah and Haggai
Tuesday	Zechariah 1–4
Wednesday	Zechariah 5-8
Thursday	Zechariah 9–11
Friday	Zechariah 12–14
Saturday	Malachi 1–4

Congratulations! You've finished the Old Testament!

BIBLE READING QUESTIONS/THOUGHTS

_____
_____
_____
_____
_____
_____
_____
_____
_____
_____

PRAYER NEEDS THIS WEEK

_____
_____
_____
_____
_____
_____
_____
_____
_____

12

Self-Evaluation 2

Fill out this self-evaluation and then compare it to Self-Evaluation 1, which you filled out in Week 1.

1. My relationship with the Lord is

distant   1   2   3   4   5   6   7   8   9   10   *intimate*

2. My experience in sharing the gospel is

nonexistent   1   2   3   4   5   6   7   8   9   10   *frequent*

3. My love and concern for others is

weak   1   2   3   4   5   6   7   8   9   10   *strong*

4. My awareness of missions is

very little   1   2   3   4   5   6   7   8   9   10   *very great*

5. My understanding of God's plan for my life is

very little   1   2   3   4   5   6   7   8   9   10   *very great*

6. My willingness to make sacrifices for the kingdom of God is

nonexistent   1   2   3   4   5   6   7   8   9   10   *sincere*

WITH KNOWLEDGE COMES RESPONSIBILITY

Yesterday I saw an accident. The motorcyclist wasn't badly hurt, but pieces of his bike lay on the ground around the van he had just hit. He stood over the ruined motorcycle, and I'm sure he said a few things I can't print here. People were running to the scene from all sides. Why? Because they were witnesses to an accident and felt a responsibility to help. If they had been on another street and weren't aware of the accident, they wouldn't have even known help was needed. But with knowledge comes responsibility.

Proverbs 24:11–12

_____

_____

We would consider people coldhearted if they saw the motorcyclist lying on the ground and drove right by without even seeing how badly he might have been hurt. Even though the entire human race is infected with the selfishness of our sinful nature, still we realize that helping others is the right thing. We do so out of an unconscious understanding of the Golden Rule. We would want others to stop and help if we had been in the accident, so we help people in the hope that when our time of need comes, someone else will be there for us.

I looked at the situation, realized the rider's injuries were minor, saw how many others had stopped to help, and understood that I wasn't needed there. So I kept driving.

There are two applications of this experience to our lives as Christians.

First, God holds us accountable for what we know. If we lived on an island without contact with the rest of the world, we would have no responsibility to share the gospel with them. That isn't the case for us, but we tend to snuggle into a comfortable Christian cocoon and ignore what we do know. If you have been on a mission outreach, you are privileged above most of the body of Christ in that you have seen firsthand some of the needs of the poor and unsaved around the world. Studying and experiencing missions is a dangerous thing—it means you have more responsibility to take action. But would you prefer ignorance? If God's heart breaks, knowing that millions die each year without a relationship with His Son, would you rather know this and share in God's heart or miss out on what is so important to Him?

James 4:17

_____

_____

Second, where there are enough people to get the job done, we're not needed there. We may be badly needed somewhere else. If you're called to be a pastor, maybe you shouldn't start a church in your own country. Why not start one in Afghanistan, which has forty-eight thousand Muslim mosques but not one Christian church building? Many people in North America are trained and gifted as worship leaders, children's workers, and teachers. But often they don't have the vision to take their gifts overseas, where the need is greatest and there are far fewer trained Christian leaders. Do you have vision to be useful to God far away?

Matthew 9:38

_____

_____

Rights vs. Responsibilities

"I have the right to . . ."

"We demand our rights."

"Equal rights for all!"

"Our rights are being violated."

Everybody wants his or her rights. The apostle Paul used half a chapter in the Bible to write about all he was entitled to have and all his rights. Then he said he gave up all of them for the sake of the gospel.

1 Corinthians 9:15–16

_____

_____

Jesus certainly had the right to be pampered and could have ordered the disciples to wait on Him, but He never did so.

Matthew 20:25–28

_____

_____

Sometimes when the Lord comes to stake His claim on our lives, we balk and complain. We may be so busy thinking of our rights that we forget about His rights. Doesn't God, as our Creator, have the right to tell us what to do? Doesn't Jesus, as our Redeemer, have the right to expect an attitude of gratitude when He wants us to do something? Doesn't God have the right to receive glory from the human race instead of being dishonored by sin, rebellion, and blasphemy all day long?

Isaiah 52:5

_____

_____

We were on a flight from Bangkok to Bombay, which is now called Mumbai. The plane had just landed, and people were getting up from their seats. An Indian man traveling with his family was enraged about something his wife and children had done. Standing just a few feet away, I heard an impressive tirade of cursing in a language I didn't understand. The intent of his words was clear. His

True Story

At this moment I'm in a favela in Rio de Janeiro, Brazil. *Favela* is the Portuguese name for slums that cover the mountainsides. One family simply builds a house up the hill from another, with a few steps leading up to it, or even buys space on the roof of the first home to build their own. The result is a maze of narrow alleys and up to eight hundred steps winding up the mountainside, with few roads and no central planning. The favelas are known for being centers of drug abuse and are usually run by a local drug lord. The government has a process of conquering these areas by sending in large numbers of military police to "pacify" the favelas and clear out the drug gangs. This one was not yet pacified. We had no problems and didn't see guns or gang activity. Most people who live in favelas are not criminals but simply the working poor, and the drug lords keep order as the government there.

This favela was fascinating—a place I would love to spend more time in. Very colorful, lively, packed with people walking down narrow but brightly lit alleys, all paved, with no trash on the ground but walls covered in graffiti. Shops and markets are full of produce, music is blaring, barefoot children play, and wheelbarrows move things around, but very few cars or trucks are inside. The entrance is guarded by a man, probably working for the local drug lord, who regulates those allowed to come in.

Each day we're in different favelas, proclaiming the message of the gospel. Now we're in a pacified favela. A few minutes ago a heavily armed patrol in bulletproof vests walked through, pausing to observe the strange sight of a group of Americans coloring Bible story pages with barefoot children. These kids love to have fun as much as others anywhere we've been in the world. A favorite diversion is kite flying at the top of the mountains, and some flatten two-liter soda bottles to use as makeshift sleds as they slide down erosion-controlling cement slopes on the mountainside.

We were very impressed with a particular favela pastor and his love for the community that twenty thousand people call home. He is a joyous and energetic man who knows everybody. People come out of the house to greet him as he walks through the narrow alleys. He pauses to pray and sing Christian songs with the children all through the favela. All the kids know the songs from the singing pastor's previous visits. The team made many stops with him and prayed with people in their homes. We put on Vacation Bible Schools for rowdy children and held outdoor evangelistic services, sharing the hope Jesus brings with throngs of beautiful kids.

Thinking about the future of these children is sobering. Many will end up in the drug and prison cycle common in favela life. We were told a common question to ask when meeting a teenage girl is "How many children do you have?" The kids of these kids will likely all have different fathers. It's the same around the world, as we were told while working with a maternity clinic in the Philippines (see page 105), where the usual sequence of events is that children born today will return in fourteen years to bear their own children.

What can break the cycle? Education and job skill training can help with the poverty, rehab centers can help free drug-addled minds, soup kitchens can give people strength to keep going another day, and vaccinations can protect their health, but only Jesus can change their hearts and give them eternal hope. Who will tell them about Him? I leave the challenge to you.

Hindu wife, with a bindi dot on her forehead and traditional clothes, stood meekly as he blasted her and the children. Then he threw out his arms and yelled in English, "Jesus Christ!"

Isn't it amazing that even the unsaved recognize that the name of Jesus is more powerful than any other? No one ever curses by Shiva, Ganesh, Hanuman, Allah, Buddha, Guanyin, or Matsu.

Exodus 20:7

_____

_____

However, in a roundabout way, when people curse with Jesus' name or add the word *God* to other profanity, they are acknowledging His power. Despite the fact that it's not done in love, submission, and honor, they still proclaim that He is great.

Psalm 76:10

_____

_____

The Lord has the right to receive honor from all people. He is worth this response. Our English word *worship* comes from *worth:* God is worth honoring. All people should freely, respectfully, and consistently give Him honor. It's the right thing to do. It's not right that "gods" who are not God should dilute and misdirect the worship of humankind.

Ask yourself some questions: Are God's rights greater than my rights? Do God's rights result in my having responsibilities? Have I ever looked at the responsibilities I have as a Christian, both to the Lord and to this lost world?

You may have had some missions experience and seen desperate poverty, helped the poor, and shared the gospel. You know that your time, effort, and money were well spent. You have a sense of accomplishment and expanded vision of needs around the world. With the things you have seen, do you have responsibility to take action? Right now you may not be able to foresee your future past high school or college graduation, but God has it figured out. Does your future include time overseas?

Proverbs 23:26

_____

_____

Let's take a look at this subject from a different perspective. Throughout this book we've looked at many reasons to serve in other countries. Now let's look at three possible reasons to serve at home.

1. "God has told me my place is in my own country." It is perfectly legitimate to say that God has called you to be an insurance salesman, a restaurant manager, a police officer, a stay-at-home mom, or any number of other professions. God calls people to stay in the United States, and He blesses people with success in business, nice homes, and comforts. He just doesn't want us to devote our lives to gaining those things. We belong to Him.

Likewise, a call to the ministry in America is valid. You may become a pastor, worship leader, or youth and children's minister in the United States, but you'll be one with a heart for the lost world. It's a legitimate role in missions to mobilize the troops for action, much as an army recruiter signs up new soldiers. Once you have gained God's heart for a lost world, it comes out in everything you do. It's no longer a side issue or annual preaching topic but rather the substance of the church's duty while we're still on earth. It invades and pervades structures and functions in every department of the church. It will crowd out lesser priorities, rearrange plans, restructure budgets, curb selfishness, and keep focus.

The solemnity of eternity will minimize petty bickering about insignificant issues and keep people from becoming idle and introspective. Mission vision permeates the church with a sense of purpose that manifests itself in confidence, action, and appeal to lost sheep needing a Shepherd.

John 4:35

_____

_____

2. "I like it here." This is the most common reason Christians stay in North America. The comforts of home, the nine-to-five predictability, and the lures of materialism and recreation make the choice easy. We love our comforts and conveniences, don't we? We *all* like it here. But have we given God the choice to assign us somewhere else?

Without making too many comments, let's just look at the Scriptures. Matthew, Mark, Luke, and John all quoted Jesus on the selfish life.

True Story

We split into pairs and loaded up on Spanish New Testaments. Another village in central Mexico lay before us, and we ignored the bad weather, going from house to house. Knocking on the door of one dilapidated shack, we were welcomed inside by a woman carrying a bundle of rags. Immediately we heard the most horrific noises coming from the bundle of rags. One shock led to the next as we realized the family lived in a chicken coop, with a low wall separating the birds from the bed and woodstove. The air was thick with fowl odors. (Sorry, I couldn't resist!) Gasping, desperate choking sounds continued from within the rags the woman held. The sense of death was heavy—I had never felt anything like it. I had never heard noises that awful. It was a nightmarish moment as I asked to see inside and the woman pulled back the blankets to show a scrawny baby girl, trying desperately to breathe.

The woman told us her baby was four months old and had been like that since birth. The baby's name was Angelica, and I asked to hold her. Our son was about the same age, and I knew how much a baby that age should weigh. Angelica hardly weighed more than the dirty rags that covered her. We knew the chicken coop environment was a factor in her health and that she couldn't survive much longer. We spoke with the woman, asked to pray for the baby, and left a New Testament. Going outside, I stopped my witnessing partner and did something I've never done before or since: we laid hands on the house and commanded the spirit of death to depart from there. That may sound overly dramatic, but you weren't there that day!

As we left the village and for the rest of the trip, I couldn't get the baby off my mind. Throughout the next school year I prayed for Angelica and asked God to show His mercy to the family. I wondered if she had survived. It was an entire year later when our team returned to the village. I brought Angelica a stuffed animal and took the same witnessing partner back to the street where she lived. We had a hard time finding the house at first, since they had repainted it and the chickens now had their own home outside the house. I was trembling when the mother came out to greet us with a toddler in her arms, and I could hardly ask if it was Angelica. It was! Her mom said, "From the day that you prayed for her, she started to get well, and within three months she was completely healthy. She has been well ever since!" Glory to Jesus, who is the Giver of life!

Matthew 16:24–26

_____

_____

Mark 4:18–19

_____

_____

Luke 9:23–25

_____

_____

John 12:24–26

_____

_____

3. "I don't know what God wants me to do yet." That's fine! He just wants you to surrender all the possibilities to Him. A person with a yielded heart will never miss God's best for his or her life. God will lead you all the way through. The only thing to watch for is the subtle process of giving God only a few possibilities—the ones you like—and deciding that His will must be one of those. But as long as your heart is true in seeking the Lord, you can be assured He will make His will known to you.

Psalm 37:23

_____

_____

Hebrews 13:20–21

_____

_____

Sign the Contract

Picture this scene in heaven. The prophet Isaiah was suddenly yanked from earth into the presence of God. Magnificent angels with six wings hovered around the throne, praising God continually. There before the Lord in all of His majesty, Isaiah was struck by his own sinfulness. An angel came to bring him forgiveness from the altar of God.

Isaiah 6:1–8

_____

_____

When God called, Isaiah responded immediately. How many people would have said, "Not me, Lord. It's too dangerous . . . uncomfortable . . . dirty . . . hard . . . scary . . . far . . ." or some other excuse?

Those answers may get by on earth, but how will they sound in heaven when we stand before the same throne Isaiah did, before the saints and martyrs of all the ages, and try to explain saying no to the Lord?

Notice how very simple Isaiah's answer was. "Here I am. Send me." He didn't say, "Now wait a minute, Lord. Go where? And for how long? How much will You pay? Give me the details and we'll negotiate."

Helper of persecuted Christians to come alongside ill-treated brothers and sisters in the body of Christ. Preferably someone who will commit to intercession, sustained monetary giving, and writing letters of encouragement to the victims' families.

Today, there are over two hundred million Christians worldwide who face persecution for their faith. These Christians endure suffering that most people in the Western world cannot imagine. Young children are refused entry to school, families are forced to live on the outskirts of their cities, pastors are imprisoned and brutally tortured, and countless believers willingly face death. Thousands of other people are indirectly affected by persecution, such as families who fight to survive after husbands or fathers are martyred. In some countries, parents who refuse to renounce Jesus have their children taken away from them and given to a family who follows Islam or Hinduism. These Christian families face greater sacrifice than what seems possible to bear. While the nature of persecution and underground churches makes it hard to find exact statistics, we can look at numbers in individual countries:

- 25 percent of the 400,000 Christians in North Korea are in labor camps for refusing to pay homage to the late Kim Il-Sung. Many remaining Christians are along the border of China, their main food being grass and bark.
- Out of 9.6 million people, there are only five known Christians in Somalia. Christians live in great secrecy due to fear of being beheaded.
- In Algeria, a Christian spent five years in prison for giving his neighbor a CD with Christian music.

It's easy to detach our emotions from the gruesome realities of the persecuted church, yet if you have been adopted into the family of God, these people are your brothers and sisters! Ask God to make their sufferings very real to you so that you are driven to your knees in intercession and faith. Decide to act on their behalf—to preach the gospel where there is no persecution, to financially support the families of those who are imprisoned, and to write government officials and plead for the release of the people who courageously refuse to deny Christ.

Rhiannon Roberts was fourteen years old when she read about the persecuted church. The stories and statistics affected her strongly, and she asked God what she should do for Christians in closed nations. After attending a conference with her dad, Rhiannon had an idea. She and a friend decided to meet monthly to pray for the persecuted church, and they invited eight other teenagers. During these meetings, the group looked at the Voice of the Martyrs website (*www.persecution.com*), prayed over people who were listed, and then did a project to benefit persecuted people. For example, Rhiannon and her friends made parachutes filled with Christian literature that were then dropped over Colombia. Additionally, Rhiannon sent out a weekly newsletter to friends, church members, and homeschool groups with specific prayer requests for persecuted people. Since then, she has been asked to speak at homeschool conventions, missions conferences, and local King's Kids events about the persecuted church.

It's your world—do something today!

Write a letter to an imprisoned Christian. Go to *www.prisoneralert.com* to encourage someone with Scripture and hope. Additionally, help support the families of people in prison by donating to *www.persecution.org/assistance*. This organization will provide food and legal aid to women and children whose primary breadwinner has been either imprisoned or martyred.

Think about signing a contract. It's wise to read every detail to make sure the other person is being fair and that you won't be legally bound to anything unpleasant in the future. We're told not to leave anything blank when we sign a contract because the other person might fill it in later with something we wouldn't want.

But we're not talking about a contract with a human being who may be dishonest or unfair. We're talking about committing our future to do whatever God wants, even though we don't know yet what that will mean. Will you follow Jesus wherever His will takes you? Do you need details of God's plan, or will you trust Him enough to sign the contract without knowing everything in advance? Is He the kind of Person who would trick you and abuse your trust in Him?

The book of Revelation describes the victory of the Lamb of God and "the ones who follow the Lamb wherever He goes" (Revelation 14:4).

Revelation 17:14

_____

_____

Called, chosen, and faithful! If there are any words I ever want to hear from the Lord besides "Well done, good and faithful servant. Enter into the joy of the Lord," it would be that He labels me called, chosen, and faithful. Many He calls don't respond. Those who do respond are chosen to complete part of the most important task in history. Then it's up to us to be faithful.

Matthew 22:14

_____

_____

The call of God to "go" cuts through the "looking out for number one" lifestyle of the world. It calls us to replace lower priorities with eternal ones. As the Lord looks down on this planet full of needs and pain, He asks the same question of you as He did Isaiah: "Who will go? Whom shall I send?" What will you reply to Him?

WRAP-UP

Let's wrap this up and apply it to our own lives. Let's put the illustrations of the motorcycle accident and the contract into a fresh prayer that sums up all we have seen this week.

Father, I've now seen and studied enough that I can't claim to be ignorant. I know many things need to be done, and many are outside the boundaries of my own country. I am willing to take on my responsibility to see that Your rights are respected. Will You show me what to do? Will You guide my steps? I'm ready to lay down my rights to live out my own will and fulfill my own plans. What are Your plans for me, Lord? I will trust You enough to leave the choices for my future up to You. Show me what You want from me, Lord. I don't know where things could go from here, but I know You are faithful and true. May my life bring You the honor You deserve. In Jesus' name. Amen.

What stands out to you in this prayer?

_____

_____

How will you put it into practice?

_____

_____

What has God been saying to you this week?

_____

_____

How does this affect your daily life?

_____

_____

How does this affect your life plans?

_____

_____

COURSE EVALUATION: *Knowing God's Heart*

Name _____ Age _____

Date _____

Please answer completely and honestly.

1. What has IDC done for your walk with the Lord?

2. What was the most beneficial part of the course?

3. What was the least beneficial part of the course?

4. What would you change about the course?

5. Were you disappointed in any aspect of the course? Explain.

6. Please comment about the following aspects of the course. How important and valuable were they to you?

    •   The amount of reading and homework:

    •   The teachings:

7. Please provide us with a quote we can use to advertise the course the next time it is offered.

Thanks for your help!
Please photocopy and mail to
Vinnie Carafano, 936 W Sunset Rd., El Paso, TX 79922

RESOURCES

YOU'VE FINISHED twelve weeks of challenge. Here are some resources to help you continue growing and learning. Don't stop challenging yourself!

Understanding Human Trafficking

God is working in the hearts of many committed Christian young adults to give them His concern for human trafficking victims. Human trafficking is an area of justice that motivates us to action through shocking statistics and nightmarish ramifications in the lives of millions worldwide.

Definition

Human trafficking is the illegal trade of human beings through force, coercion, or other means for the purposes of commercial sexual exploitation, forced labor, reproductive slavery, or other forms of slavery.

Related Scripture

The Old Testament law against kidnapping was extremely severe, showing just how much it is against God's will. The prophets highlighted God's desire for justice, and the New Testament reflects on the root of evil, including injustices like trafficking.

Exodus 21:16 He who kidnaps a man and sells him, or if he is found in his hand, shall surely be put to death.

Deuteronomy 24:7 If a man is found kidnapping any of his brethren of the children of Israel, and mistreats him or sells him, then that kidnapper shall die; and you shall put away the evil from among you.

Isaiah 58:6 Is this not the fast that I have chosen: to loose the bonds of wickedness, to undo the heavy burdens, to let the oppressed go free, and that you break every yoke?

1 Timothy 1:9–10 The law is not made for a righteous person, but . . . for fornicators, for sodomites, for kidnappers, for liars, for perjurers, and if there is any other thing that is contrary to sound doctrine.

1 Timothy 6:10 For the love of money is a root of all kinds of evil, for which some have strayed from the faith in their greediness, and pierced themselves through with many sorrows.

Types of Exploitation

Not all trafficking is sex trafficking. Human trafficking victims include domestic servants, farm laborers, carpet factory workers in India and Pakistan, child soldiers (especially in Africa), and families working off impossible debts in many nations. Other types of exploitation include the harvesting and sale of organs for medical purposes, child brides, forced begging, and surrogate motherhood.

How Does Human Trafficking Happen?

Criminal recruiters use various means to trap new victims. Here we will focus on typical ways of sex trafficking:

Recruiters offer "help" to young girls looking for jobs as models, dancers, or restaurant workers. Travel agencies, dating agencies, and study-abroad programs are also used as means of meeting prospects. The Internet, ads on college campuses, and personal contact are common means of solicitation. Exploitation of orphans, sale by family members, and kidnapping round out the approaches to the modern-day slave trade.

Potential victims often fail to heed red flags, such as being offered too high a salary for the work expected, glamorous depictions of working in another country, being told to keep the job offer a secret, hearing too few details of the job description or housing, or using false documents to cross borders.

From this point, targeted women and children, as well as some men, enter a web of criminal smugglers and are often transported across borders. Forced addiction to drugs, terror, and emotional manipulation break the will of the now victimized and enslaved and complete the web of control over their lives.

STATISTICS

Global statistics

- There are an estimated 21 million slaves worldwide.
- Human trafficking is a $32 billion annual industry.
- Human trafficking is the fastest growing criminal industry in the world.
- 80 percent of trafficked victims are women and children.
- 70 percent of women are trafficked for the sex trade.
- There are as many as 2 million children in the global sex trade.
- Major sports events such as the World Cup are prime locations for human trafficking. An estimated 10,000 prostitutes, including underage girls, worked at a recent Super Bowl.

US statistics

- Sex trafficking is a $7 billion business in the United States.
- 100,000 to 300,000 American children are trafficked within the United States each year; some are sold by parents for drug money.
- Some 2 million children run away from home annually; one-third are believed to be lured or recruited by traffickers within 48 hours.
- The average age of entry into sex trafficking for girls is between twelve and fourteen. For boys, the average entry age is between eleven and thirteen.
- A prostituted child is forced to serve 100 to 1,500 clients per year.
- The states with the most activity are Texas, Nevada, California, and New York. The United States is one of the top three destination points in the world for victims.
- Clients are often businessmen, doctors, and lawyers who can pay $3,000 to $5,000 per hour for a nine-year-old virgin girl. Some online sites sell young people for as low as $40.
- There are fewer than thirty safe homes for victims of sex trafficking in the United States.

FIRSTHAND OBSERVATIONS

Throughout this book, you've seen repeated emphasis on injustices and heartbreaking situations:

- A six-year-old sexual abuse victim in Ecuador (pages 72–73)
- A dancer in the OfficeMax parking lot (page 77)
- Russian orphans and life on the streets there (page 60). 600,000 orphans in Russia are at risk for futures in street crime, prostitution, drug smuggling, and the Mafia.
- Street children in Paraguay (page 131)

We have witnessed many other injustices and have been told about others by missionaries in countries where we minister. Here are a few:

Haitian kids are often expected to pay for doctor visits and official papers for school through sex. A Haitian child can sell for as little as $150 in a traditional system of household laborers called *restaveks*. Up to 300,000 Haitian children suffer from harsh labor and sexual abuse in this form of slavery.

Many children and teenagers are among the 100,000 homeless people on the streets of Addis Ababa, the capital of **Ethiopia**. Girls on the street face a constant threat of rape. Stronger teenage boys who are able to fight to protect them often have three to four "street wives," yet can't provide for them financially until they send them out as prostitutes. When we were there in 2004, the price of a child prostitute on the street was three birr—36 cents! This is one of the reasons that AIDS is rampant in Ethiopia.

Ukraine is an example of the worst issues of human trafficking, and all of **Eastern Europe** is similar. Poverty makes many youth vulnerable to exploitation. We heard about fraudulent ads put up at Ukrainian universities for cruise ship jobs in **Belarus** as well as slave traders offering jobs at Disney World in order to lure girls into settings from which they can be captured and trafficked. Traffickers go to villages and offer naive girls waitressing jobs in Kiev, and the girls disappear into the web of slavery. These scams lure thousands of young women into international forced prostitution. About 500,000 Ukrainian women have been trafficked, and ads featuring Ukrainian prostitutes even appear in **Tokyo**.

Statistics for orphans in Ukraine graduating at age sixteen are grim:

- 73 percent will not find work.
- 70 percent of boys will end up in crime.
- 60 percent of girls will become prostitutes.
- 10 percent will commit suicide.
  (Source: YWAM Kiev, 2011)

There is an unforgettable video on YouTube called "Stella's Voice" by PCMinistries, showing the plight of trafficked orphan girls sold for $1,500 in **Moldova**. A staggering 10 percent of the entire population of the country has been trafficked (*Nefarious*, 2011).

Julie Carafano writes: "In the **Czech Republic**, I came across this prostituted woman waiting for cars to come by. Before she got into another car I went up to her and asked if I could pray for her. A lot of the time, the prostitutes wouldn't talk to us or respond to us, but this time, the woman did. She said, 'All I want to know is that there is love. I know that it's out there, but I haven't found it yet.' It was such a profound thing to me because she knew that there was real love and that she hadn't found it yet. So to pray with her and look her in the eye, to say that she was beautiful and that God loved her, it made a difference in her life that night. After we prayed, she still went back to work, but it gave me hope and the revelation that these women are still searching for something. When God puts a burden on our hearts, we're able to show them that God does love them and that He cares about their lives."

In **Hong Kong**, signs in tourist areas advertise "rainbow girls," presumably those of every color. Prostitution bars and street markets with sexual apparatuses draw crowds of men to trafficked young **Nepali** girls.

The Philippines is one of the world's centers for sexual tourism, in which planeloads of men from wealthier countries come for sex vacations to take advantage of trafficked girls from poor villages. The sources of these tours are primarily the US, Australia, Japan, and Korea. Signs saying, "GRE [guest

Determined Christians to seek justice and redemption for men, women, and children bought and sold in the global sex trade.

For this section, we will spotlight Julie Carafano, Vinnie's daughter and Kristin's sister. In high school, Julie loved to experiment with makeup and hair and earned her cosmetology license. Her dream was to have a modeling career and use her license in California. In 2009 she graduated from high school and went on a King's Kids outreach to the Philippines. Julie learned about human trafficking there through meeting and ministering to prostitutes. She began to understand the horror of modern-day slavery.

Julie went on a YWAM Discipleship Training School to Thailand and later to the Czech Republic and Romania. She witnessed red-light districts and built relationships with trafficked teenagers, transvestite prostitutes, and gypsies. She saw that the people were beautiful but broken, with nothing to live for except prostitution and addictions. Julie had the idea to use her practical skill in cosmetology and advertised free haircuts for the local people. On the first day, pimps brought in twenty-six prostituted women! The pimps trusted the women to get haircuts by themselves, and so an amazing thing happened: They left the women alone in Julie's makeshift salon. Julie had uninterrupted, unmonitored time to counsel them through prayer and the message of Jesus.

God has given Julie a dream to take cosmetology and turn it into a ministry. She is majoring in business while working at a local salon. She plans to move to India and start a salon near a red-light district while opening a cosmetology school to train rescued women. Her mission statement is to embrace, redeem, and value the restoration of beauty to prostituted women so that through their redeemed hearts, they can help redeem others. Julie is combining two of her passions (cosmetology and redemption for women) to honor God and change her world.

We don't have to fit a generic definition of a missionary. Look at your skills and ask God how you can use them to glorify Him. He is a creative God and can use things that we love as tools to evangelize and bind up broken hearts.

In Julie's words

"Where do we come in? Our first response may be anger. I know mine was. Many of you guys may want to hurt every pimp you see. I've seen men buy out my friends— I understand. However, that is *not* God's heart for the situation. These men and women who are buying and trafficking need Jesus just as much as the prostitutes and child slaves need Him. They need Jesus just as much as we do. They are hurt people who are addicted to sin and dead in their sin *just like we were*. God is a God of justice and mercy, kindness and severity. Our heart must be both, not just one. There is a righteous anger that God gives us toward the situation.

"What if you still feel weird about relating to this? Remember they were kids once, just like you. Dreams of a future, dreams of a family, dreams of a Prince Charming, etc. Jesus loves them just like He loves you and me. It's our responsibility to show them that love. You may be the only person who shows them love in their *entire* life. Don't have a mind-set of them being dirty or unclean. Don't stare or feel nervous. If they are able to talk, they most likely want to. Our testimony is God's restoration of our lives. We all need a Savior and freedom, just like them. We have the hope and future they need."

Even younger teenagers can get involved. At age fourteen, Adriel Morgan caught the vision of trafficked women from Julie. At fifteen Adriel led a group from her high school to raise funds and collect toiletries for a local trafficking shelter and developed a class project for them that made it to third place in her state. She also co-led a workshop with Julie for thirty-five teenagers and adults, which led to a project to gather clothing for the shelter. Adriel and Adam Drake held workshops at two youth conferences for two hundred youth to alert them to trafficking.

Adam was a high school junior when he and Adriel pioneered a "Removing the Barcode" group on Facebook, and a summer outreach to Ukraine solidified his concern for trafficked orphans. He helped write and acted in a drama that his team presented to hundreds of Ukrainian people to help them understand trafficking. At the time of this writing, Adam is in a training school with YWAM in Ukraine.

It's your world—do something today!

Get involved locally: Alongside your parents, call a battered women's shelter and ask if you can bring in a homemade dinner. While there, listen to the women's stories, play with their children, and point them to redemption in Christ.

Get involved internationally: Ask your high school if you can sell concessions at a football game, and donate the money to the International Justice Mission, a group that has brought freedom to over one thousand sex slaves in four countries. Visit *www.ijm.org* for more information.

relations officer or prostitute] can earn up to $800/month!" encourage desperate young women to sell their bodies and souls, and an incentive system in the red-light district offers small appliances after time in the business. This is very significant to girls who come from villages that don't even have electricity! One woman told Kristin that she had already received a microwave. Her comments ended with, "I'm going for the refrigerator!"

In **India**, desperately poor families sell little girls as *devadasis*, or brides of the gods, to work as Hindu temple prostitutes. One of my former youth group girls received her degree as a nurse and applied to her denomination as a medical missionary. She was told her first assignment would be to their home for these girls, who are abandoned on the street at age seven or eight when they contract AIDS. The home takes them in, loves them, and ministers to them until they die. I cannot imagine a more heartbreaking ministry.

Thailand is the global capital of the sex trade, with many young girls trafficked from **Burma** (Myanmar) and **China**. In the appropriately named Fang district in northern Thailand, villages find wealth by exchanging their young children for money. The trade-off is the innocence of the next generation for flush toilets, cars, and nicer homes. One village my daughter visited had only three little girls left after selling the rest. There's also great demand for "ladyboys" who are surgically altered or transvestite males. Most don't get an education, have no skills outside of prostitution, and never escape slavery. In Thai culture prostitution is seen as a legitimate occupation. One hundred thousand German men visit Thailand on sex tours each year.

When the tourism authority of Thailand dubbed 1987 "Visit Thailand Year," its slogan was: "The one fruit of Thailand more delicious than durian [a native fruit]—its young women."

One of the most unforgettable days I've ever had was right across the border in Juárez, **Mexico**, which I can see from my backyard. We started by touring a home for ex-prostituted and heroin-addicted girls, mostly ages thirteen or fourteen. Seeing these children—*children!*—and understanding their background left us speechless. Next was prayer by the bedside of a dying prostitute in the red-light district, as AIDS took its toll. The ministry we worked with goes out every Thursday night to take burritos, songs, and a gospel message to the prostitutes. As I stood watching, a surgically enhanced young man in a leopard-print miniskirt batted his eyes at me, thinking I was a potential customer, as cars with American license plates cruised the narrow streets. It was sickening. A recent headline from this city read, "Mexico Arrests 1000 in Human Trafficking Raids—300 Police Involved in Mass Operation."

THREE MAJOR MISCONCEPTIONS

"Prostitution is a victimless crime."

It would be useless to say this to the millions ensnared by modern-day slavery. It is necessary to make a distinction between prostitution and trafficking, in that some women (or men) sell themselves to have money for drugs or food, apart from any other individual's control, but the toll of human suffering requires us to see the big picture of the prostitution industry. Many women in pornography are trafficked. All children in pornography are exploited and victimized. There are 56,000 US-produced websites that sell child pornography, and one-fifth of the images are of minors (CBN). Prostitution promotes adultery and fornication. It's linked with drug trafficking and kidnapping. There are many victims in this criminal empire.

"The women should just run away."

Here's why they stay:

- They face shame, manipulation, and emotional abuse from the pimps.
- Many don't want to leave—they have no education, job skills, or knowledge of life outside of prostitution.
- Some are literally chained in locked rooms.
- Many are working off debt. Pimps charge them for room and board, clothing, and other expenses, in addition to earlier debts. Payments made to their families in exchange for trafficking them are added to a bill that often never diminishes. By addicting them to drugs and then charging the women for them, the circle of control is complete.
- They fear lethal retaliation against themselves or family members.
- Many are trafficked across international borders. They don't speak the language of their new country and have no contacts to help them, and their passports are usually confiscated by the pimps. I have seen this firsthand in my own city.
- They are blackmailed and fear exposure to their families.
- They need money.

"There should be laws passed to stop this."

There are many laws on the books, but political will to stop slavery is lacking. The lucrative nature of the business provides ample funds to bribe corrupt officials up to the highest levels of government. According to CBN, "Only 1 out of 100,000 traffickers ever serves time for his crime." Income from sex tourism is a significant source of revenue for poor nations. An international outcry, bringing pressure on governments to enact or enforce laws against the myriad of crimes associated with human trafficking, is desperately needed. In addition, government sanctions and boycotts of the airlines, hotels, resorts, and tourist industries of nations with significant trafficking issues would provide the financial pressure needed to cause those nations to take action.

Resources

Organizations and websites

Anti-Slavery International, *www.antislavery.org*

Because Justice Matters, *www.becausejusticematters.org*

Captive Daughters, *www.captivedaughters.org*

ECPAT, *www.ecpat.net*

Free the Slaves, *www.freetheslaves.net*

Free2Play, *www.teamfree2play.org*

Free2Work, *www.free2work.org*

GoodWeave, *www.goodweave.net*

Hagar, *www.hagarinternational.org*

Hope for the Sold, *http://hopeforthesold.com*

International Justice Mission, *www.ijm.org*

Justice (ACTs), *www.justiceacts.org*

Not For Sale, *www.notforsalecampaign.org*

ProCon.org, article on prostitution, *http://prostitution.procon.org*

Save the Children, *www.savethechildren.org*

Slavery Map, *www.slaverymap.org*

Stop the Traffik, *www.stopthetraffik.org*

Movies worth seeing

Born into Brothels: a secular documentary about the children of prostitutes in Kolkata

Taken: a Hollywood movie with many accurate depictions of trafficked women

Nefarious: a Christian documentary with current information and heart-wrenching stories

An important note about human trafficking resources: Some videos show accurate but graphic depictions of the sufferings of trafficked women. These can be a stumbling block and an enticement to sin for male viewers. I urge those interested in this subject to use prayerful wisdom about avoiding such material. Be equally cautious about Internet research on prostitution lest you stumble upon or be tempted by pornography. Teenagers should have prayer support and parental accountability when studying this subject.

PRAY FOR

- justice for the oppressed;
- the traffickers themselves to come to repentance and forgiveness through Christ;
- the fear of the Lord to touch the hearts of users of trafficked people;
- an increase in the cry for justice in our hearts and our churches.

Prayer Guide: The Nations of the World

Use this list to pray for every nation. See page 170 for God's promises to draw the nations to Jesus.

Afghanistan
Albania
Algeria
American Samoa (US)
Andorra
Angola
Anguilla (UK)
Antigua & Barbuda
Argentina
Armenia
Aruba (Netherlands)
Australia
Austria
Azerbaijan
Bahamas, The
Bahrain
Bangladesh
Barbados
Belarus
Belgium
Belize
Benin
Bermuda (UK)
Bhutan
Bolivia
Bosnia & Herzegovina
Botswana
Brazil
British Virgin Is. (UK)
Brunei
Bulgaria
Burkina Faso
Burma (Myanmar)
Burundi
Cambodia
Cameroon
Canada
Cape Verde Is.
Cayman Is. (UK)

Central African Republic
Chad
Chile
China
Christmas Is. (Australia)
Cocos Is. (Australia)
Colombia
Comoros
Congo, Democratic Republic
   of the
Congo, Republic of the
Cook Is. (NZ)
Costa Rica
Côte d'Ivoire
Croatia
Cuba
Cyprus
Czech Republic
Denmark
Djibouti
Dominica
Dominican Republic
Ecuador
Egypt
El Salvador
Equatorial Guinea
Eritrea
Estonia
Ethiopia
Faeroe Is.
Falkland Is.
Fiji
Finland
France
French Guiana (France)
French Polynesia
Gabon
Gambia, The
Gaza Strip*

Georgia
Germany
Ghana
Gibraltar (UK)
Greece
Greenland (Denmark)
Grenada
Guadeloupe (France)
Guam (US)
Guatemala
Guernsey (UK)
Guinea
Guinea-Bissau
Guyana
Haiti
Honduras
Hong Kong (China)
Hungary
Iceland
India
Indonesia
Iran
Iraq
Ireland
Isle of Man (UK)
Israel
Italy
Jamaica
Japan
Jersey (UK)
Jordan
Kazakhstan
Kenya
Kiribati
Korea (North)
Korea (South)
Kuwait
Kyrgyzstan
Laos

Latvia	Northern Mariana Is. (US)	Sudan
Lebanon	Norway	Suriname
Lesotho	Oman	Svalbard (Norway)
Liberia	Pakistan	Swaziland
Libya	Palau	Sweden
Liechtenstein	Panama	Switzerland
Lithuania	Papua New Guinea	Syria
Luxembourg	Paraguay	Taiwan*
Macau (China)	Peru	Tajikistan
Macedonia	Philippines	Tanzania
Madagascar	Pitcairn Is. (UK)	Thailand
Malawi	Poland	Timor-Leste
Malaysia	Portugal	Togo
Maldives	Puerto Rico (US)	Tokelau (NZ)
Mali	Qatar	Tonga Is.
Malta	Réunion Is. (France)	Trinidad & Tobago
Marshall Is.	Romania	Tunisia
Martinique (France)	Russia	Turkey
Mauritania	Rwanda	Turkmenistan
Mauritius	Saint Barthélemy (France)	Turks & Caicos Is. (UK)
Mayotte (France)	Saint Helena (UK)	Tuvalu
Mexico	Saint Kitts & Nevis	Uganda
Federated States of Micronesia	Saint Lucia	Ukraine
Moldova	Saint Martin (Fr./Neth.)	United Arab Emirates
Monaco	Saint Pierre & Miquelon	United Kingdom
Mongolia	St. Vincent & the Grenadines	United States
Montenegro	Samoa	Uruguay
Montserrat (UK)	San Marino	Uzbekistan
Morocco	São Tomé & Príncipe	Vanuatu
Mozambique	Saudi Arabia	Vatican City
Namibia	Senegal	Venezuela
Nauru	Serbia	Vietnam
Nepal	Seychelles	Virgin Islands (US)
Netherlands	Sierra Leone	Wallis & Futuna Is. (France)
Netherlands Antilles	Singapore	West Bank*
New Caledonia (France)	Slovakia	Western Sahara*
New Zealand	Slovenia	Yemen
Nicaragua	Solomon Is.	Zambia
Niger	Somalia	Zimbabwe
Nigeria	South Africa	
Niue (NZ)	South Sudan	** The national status of this*
Norfolk Is. (Australia)	Spain	*region is undesignated.*
Northern Cyprus	Sri Lanka	

Scripture Resource: God's Promises to Draw the Nations to Jesus

Psalm 2:8 Ask of Me, and I will give You the nations for Your inheritance, and the ends of the earth for Your possession.

Psalm 22:27–28 All the ends of the world shall remember and turn to the LORD, and all the families of the nations shall worship before You. For the kingdom is the LORD's, and He rules over the nations.

Psalm 46:10 Be still, and know that I am God; I will be exalted among the nations, I will be exalted in the earth!

Psalm 47:7–8 For God is the King of all the earth; sing praises with understanding. God reigns over the nations; God sits on His holy throne.

Psalm 66:4 All the earth shall worship You and sing praises to You; they shall sing praises to Your name.

Psalm 67:1–2 God be merciful to us and bless us, and cause His face to shine upon us, that Your way may be known on earth, Your salvation among all nations.

Psalm 72:8–19 He shall have dominion also from sea to sea, and from the River to the ends of the earth. Those who dwell in the wilderness will bow before Him, and His enemies will lick the dust. . . . Yes, all kings shall fall down before Him; all nations shall serve Him. . . . His name shall endure forever; His name shall continue as long as the sun. And men shall be blessed in Him; all nations shall call Him blessed. Blessed be the LORD God, the God of Israel, who only does wondrous things! And blessed be His glorious name forever! And let the whole earth be filled with His glory. Amen and Amen.

Psalm 86:9 All nations whom You have made shall come and worship before You, O Lord, and shall glorify Your name.

Psalm 96:3 Declare His glory among the nations, His wonders among all peoples.

Psalm 105:13–15 When they went from one nation to another, from one kingdom to another people, He permitted no one to do them wrong; yes, He rebuked kings for their sakes, saying, "Do not touch My anointed ones, and do My prophets no harm."

Isaiah 11:9 For the earth shall be full of the knowledge of the LORD as the waters cover the sea.

Isaiah 40:5 The glory of the LORD shall be revealed, and all flesh shall see it together; for the mouth of the LORD has spoken.

Isaiah 45:22–23 Look to Me, and be saved, all you ends of the earth! For I am God, and there is no other. I have sworn by Myself; the word has gone out of My mouth in righteousness, and shall not return, that to Me every knee shall bow, every tongue shall take an oath.

Isaiah 49:6 Indeed He says, "It is too small a thing that You should be My Servant to raise up the tribes of Jacob, and to restore the preserved ones of Israel; I will also give You as a light to the Gentiles, that You should be My salvation to the ends of the earth."

Isaiah 52:10 The Lord has made bare His holy arm in the eyes of all the nations; and all the ends of the earth shall see the salvation of our God.

Isaiah 56:6–8 "Also the sons of the foreigner who join themselves to the Lord, to serve Him, and to love the name of the Lord, to be His servants—everyone who keeps from defiling the Sabbath, and holds fast My covenant—even them I will bring to My holy mountain, and make them joyful in My house of prayer. Their burnt offerings and their sacrifices will be accepted on My altar; for My house shall be called a house of prayer for all nations." The Lord God, who gathers the outcasts of Israel, says, "Yet I will gather to him others besides those who are gathered to him."

Micah 4:1–2 Now it shall come to pass in the latter days that the mountain of the Lord's house shall be established on the top of the mountains, and shall be exalted above the hills; and peoples shall flow to it. Many nations shall come and say, "Come, and let us go up to the mountain of the Lord, to the house of the God of Jacob; He will teach us His ways, and we shall walk in His paths." For out of Zion the law shall go forth, and the word of the Lord from Jerusalem.

Habakkuk 1:5 Look among the nations and watch—be utterly astounded! For I will work a work in your days which you would not believe, though it were told you.

Zephaniah 2:11 The Lord will be awesome to them, for He will reduce to nothing all the gods of the earth; people shall worship Him, each one from his place, indeed all the shores of the nations.

Haggai 2:7 "And I will shake all nations, and they shall come to the Desire of All Nations, and I will fill this temple with glory," says the Lord of hosts.

Zechariah 2:11 Many nations shall be joined to the Lord in that day, and they shall become My people. And I will dwell in your midst. Then you will know that the Lord of hosts has sent Me to you.

Malachi 1:11 "For from the rising of the sun, even to its going down, My name shall be great among the Gentiles; in every place incense shall be offered to My name, and a pure offering; for My name shall be great among the nations," says the Lord of hosts.

Matthew 16:18 And I also say to you that you are Peter, and on this rock I will build My church, and the gates of Hades shall not prevail against it.

Matthew 24:14 And this gospel of the kingdom will be preached in all the world as a witness to all the nations, and then the end will come.

Matthew 28:18–20 And Jesus came and spoke to them, saying, "All authority has been given to Me in heaven and on earth. Go therefore and make disciples of all the nations, baptizing them in the name of the Father and of the Son and of the Holy Spirit, teaching them to observe all things that I have commanded you; and lo, I am with you always, even to the end of the age." Amen.

Luke 2:30–32 For my eyes have seen Your salvation which You have prepared before the face of all peoples, a light to bring revelation to the Gentiles, and the glory of Your people Israel.

Luke 24:45–48 And He opened their understanding, that they might comprehend the Scriptures. Then He said to them, "Thus it is written, and thus it was necessary for the Christ to suffer and to rise from the dead the third day, and that repentance and remission of sins should be preached in His name to all nations, beginning at Jerusalem. And you are witnesses of these things."

John 12:32 And I, if I am lifted up from the earth, will draw all peoples to Myself.

Acts 1:8 But you shall receive power when the Holy Spirit has come upon you; and you shall be witnesses to Me in Jerusalem, and in all Judea and Samaria, and to the end of the earth.

Acts 13:47 For so the Lord has commanded us: "I have set you as a light to the Gentiles, that you should be for salvation to the ends of the earth."

Revelation 5:9 And they sang a new song, saying: "You are worthy to take the scroll, and to open its seals; for You were slain, and have redeemed us to God by Your blood out of every tribe and tongue and people and nation."

Revelation 7:9 After these things I looked, and behold, a great multitude which no one could number, of all nations, tribes, peoples, and tongues, standing before the throne and before the Lamb, clothed with white robes, with palm branches in their hands.

ALTERNATE DAILY BIBLE READING PLAN

If this is your first book in the Intensive Discipleship Course series, we recommend that you begin reading three to four chapters of the New Testament daily. After you have completed the New Testament, start the Old Testament. If you read the Bible for about fifteen minutes each day, you can finish it in one year. Just keep at it. If you miss a day or get behind, try to catch up and don't quit. Check off each day after you read the chapters and start the next day where you left off.

	Sunday	Monday	Tuesday	Wednesday	Thursday	Friday	Saturday
Week 1	Matthew 1–4	5–7	8–11	12–15	16–19	20–23	24–25
Week 2	26–28	Mark 1–3	4–7	8–10	11–13	14–16	Luke 1–2
Week 3	3–6	7–9	10–12	13–15	16–18	19–21	22–24
Week 4	John 1–2	3–5	6–8	9–12	13–17	18–21	Acts 1–4
Week 5	5–7	8–9	10–12	13–15	16–18	19–23	24–26
Week 6	27–28	Romans 1–3	4–5	6–8	9–11	12–16	1 Corinthians 1–6
Week 7	7–11	12–14	15–16	2 Corinthians 1–6	7–9	10–13	Galatians 1–6
Week 8	Ephesians 1–6	Philippians 1–4	Colossians 1–4	1 Thessalonians 1–5	2 Thessalonians 1–3	1 Timothy 1–3	4–6
Week 9	2 Timothy 1–4	Titus 1–3	Philemon	Hebrews 1–2	3–4	5–7	8–10
Week 10	11–13	James 1–5	1 Peter 1–5	2 Peter 1–3	1 John 1–5	2 John, 3 John	Jude
Week 11	Revelation 1–3	4–6	7–9	10–13	14–16	17–19	20–22
Week 12	Catch up if you're behind.						

RECOMMENDED READING

EVANGELISM

Chantry, Walter J. *Today's Gospel: Authentic or Synthetic?* London: Banner of Truth Trust, 1970.

Coleman, Robert E. *The Master Plan of Evangelism.* 2nd ed. abridged. Grand Rapids: Spire, 1994.

Comfort, Ray. *Hell's Best Kept Secret.* Expanded ed. New Kensington, Pa.: Whitaker House, 2004.

MISSIONS

Andrew, Brother. *God's Smuggler.* With John and Elizabeth Sherrill. Grand Rapids: Chosen Books, 2001.

Baumann, Dan. *Imprisoned in Iran: Love's Victory over Fear.* Seattle: YWAM Publishing, 2000.

Cunningham, Loren. *Daring to Live on the Edge: The Adventure of Faith and Finances.* Seattle: YWAM Publishing, 1992.

Cunningham, Loren. *Is That Really You, God? Hearing the Voice of God.* With Janice Rogers. 2nd ed. Seattle: YWAM Publishing, 2001.

Elliot, Elisabeth. *Through Gates of Splendor.* Carol Stream, Ill.: Tyndale House, 2005.

Esther, Gulshan. *The Torn Veil.* New ed. Grand Rapids: Zondervan, 2004.

Garlock, H. B. *Before We Kill and Eat You: Tales of Faith in the Face of Certain Death.* New ed. With Ruthanne Garlock. Ventura, Calif.: Regal Books, 2006.

Grant, Myrna. *Vanya.* Carol Stream, Ill.: Creation House, 1974.

Johnstone, Patrick, ed. *Praying through the Window III: The Unreached Peoples.* Seattle: YWAM Publishing, 1996.

Mandryk, Jason. *Operation World.* 7th ed. Colorado Springs: Biblica, 2010.

Olson, Bruce. *Bruchko.* Seattle: YWAM Publishing, 2005.

Otis, George, Jr., ed. *Strongholds of the 10/40 Window: Intercessor's Guide to the World's Least Evangelized Nations.* With Mark Brockman. Seattle: YWAM Publishing, 1995.

Otis, George, Jr. *The Last of the Giants: Lifting the Veil on Islam and the End Times.* Tarrytown, N.Y.: Chosen Books, 1991.

Pullinger, Jackie. *Chasing the Dragon.* Ventura, Calif.: Gospel Light, 2004.

Richardson, Don. *Eternity in Their Hearts.* New ed. Ventura, Calif.: Regal Books, 2006.

Richardson, Don. *Lords of the Earth.* Seattle: YWAM Publishing, 2003.

Richardson, Don. *Peace Child.* Seattle: YWAM Publishing, 2003.

Sjogren, Bob. *Unveiled at Last.* Seattle: YWAM Publishing, 1988.

Wagner, C. Peter, ed. *Praying through the 100 Gateway Cities of the 10/40 Window.* 2nd ed. Seattle: YWAM Publishing, 2010.

Yun, Brother. *The Heavenly Man: The Remarkable True Story of Chinese Christian Brother Yun.* With Paul Hattaway. Toronto: Monarch Books, 2002.

ABOUT THE AUTHORS

Vinnie Carafano lives in El Paso, Texas. He and his wife, Jodie, have four children: Vincent, Kimberly, Kristin, and Julie. Vinnie was the youth pastor of Jesus Chapel East for fourteen years until God called his family into King's Kids in 1993. His lifetime commitment is to see young people come into a living relationship with Jesus Christ and affect the world around them.

The Carafano family's missionary travels have taken them to India, the Philippines, Korea, Paraguay, Panama, Nicaragua, Mexico, Canada, Haiti, St. Croix, Barbados, Grenada, Jamaica, Russia, Ethiopia, Ecuador, Taiwan, Thailand, China, Iraq, Turkey, Lebanon, Romania, the Czech Republic, Ukraine, Brazil, and throughout the United States.

Kristin Carafano is Vinnie and Jodie's daughter. She wrote all of the Help Wanted sections of this book. Kristin recently graduated from university with a degree in Family and Child Development. She currently lives in Texas, where she teaches in a Christian school, works part-time with Christ Community Church, and helps lead worship. Kristin plans to go into full-time ministry with her church and aims to work with children living in crisis.

More volumes in the

Intensive Discipleship Course

You did it! After three months of studying the Word and seeking the Lord, you are not the same person you were when you started. We hope your hunger for God continues. Here are other steps in the Intensive Discipleship Course for continued learning and growth.

Developing Godly Character

This is the foundation of the Intensive Discipleship Course—an intense twelve weeks of spiritual growth, with twelve powerful messages on how you can become who God wants you to be. You'll learn how to study the Bible effectively, develop a strong prayer life, serve in humility, overcome sin, and grow spiritually.
ISBN 978-1-57658-410-1

Being Useful to God Now

Ready to put your faith into action? This volume is all about serving God and others—right now, right where you're at in life. You'll learn how to be an active, effective disciple of Christ by modeling God's love and compassion, studying evangelism techniques, preparing Bible studies, counseling peers through life-controlling problems, and hearing God's call on your life.
ISBN 978-1-57658-470-5

Reaching a Lost World: Cults and World Religions

What would you say to a Muslim friend who says Jesus was just a prophet? How would you expose the deception in the beliefs of Mormon missionaries? Could you answer the arguments of Jehovah's Witnesses at your door? Could you explain or defend the doctrine of the Trinity or the validity of the Bible? This volume will challenge you to dig deeply into the Word of God for answers to these questions and many more. In twelve weeks you'll be equipped as a more effective witness for the Lord.
ISBN 978-1-57658-499-6

Available at your local Christian bookstore or from YWAM Publishing
www.ywampublishing.com
1-800-922-2143